"This inspiring book is a must read for women in ministry or those who want a deeper understanding of their spiritual journey. Dr. Mary Paul offers brilliant insights into the soul of ministry and the unique challenges as well as the blessings that women experience in their obedience to God's call to pastoral ministry."

—Maggie Bailey
Vice Provost Graduate Studies
Point Loma Nazarene University

"Dr. Paul's approach is not a journey into feministic bitterness or derisive accusations, but a grace-filled pilgrimage into biblical hope as she points to Jesus and His raising up of the daughter of Jairus as 'a call for all of us who have fallen asleep to the point of death, to open our eyes, to awaken. Rise up daughter; There is more for you to do.'"

—Kenneth L. Mills
District Superintendent
Mid-Atlantic District Church of the Nazarene

"Dr. Paul has written a powerful and bold book that will greatly impact and enhance the cross-gender understanding on women in pastoral leadership. . . . The message of the book is relevant and needed in our current Christian environment and culture."

—Dr. Jossie E. Owens
Former District Superintendent
New England District

# WOMEN WHO LEAD

## THE CALL OF WOMEN IN MINISTRY

MARY REARICK PAUL

BEACON HILL PRESS
OF KANSAS CITY

### Library of Congress Cataloging-in-Publication Data

Paul, Mary (Mary Rearick)
    Women who lead : the call of women in ministry / Mary Paul.
        p. cm.
    Includes bibliographical references.
    ISBN 978-0-8341-2564-3 (pbk.)
    1. Women clergy. I. Title.
    BV676.P298 2011
    253.082—dc22

                                                                    2010047684

10 9 8 7 6 5 4 3 2 1

# DEDICATION

To Bruce, my companion in ministry, life, and love.

# CONTENTS

*Acknowledgments*     9

*Introduction*     11

ONE
A Story of Hope for All     15

TWO
Deeper Resurrection     26

THREE
We Need Women Leaders     37

FOUR
God's Song of Praise     47

FIVE
The Healing of the Leader     58

SIX
Receiving Power     70

SEVEN
Toxicity of Power     81

EIGHT
Necessary Blend     93

NINE
Servant Leader     108

TEN
Women's Ways of Leading     121

ELEVEN
Obstacles     132

TWELVE
Necessary Qualities     140

*Notes*     149

# ACKNOWLEDGMENTS

I have been blessed beyond reason with incredible support through the process of writing this book. I would like to thank my husband, Bruce, and my sons, Wesley and JJ. They have given up much to provide the space, time, and resources needed to complete this project. Bruce's faith in me, his support, and his love are invaluable in my life.

When I began pondering a theme for my dissertation, which then expanded and grew into this book, I was warned by a friend not to focus on women. His concern was that I would be pigeonholed as a person with only one interest. I understood those concerns, and while I see my interests as pastor and leader to be broad in scope, there is an ongoing story of a Christian woman's need for greater space to live out her freedom in Christ. I have now been leading long enough to have mentored and encouraged a younger generation of women to believe the church (both parish and para-church organizations), despite its hesitancy, would embrace them and their gifts. Some have flourished, and I give great thanks. Others have not, and it has grieved my heart to have them return with questions about the suffering they have endured. I could not stay away from this topic, because I continue to live and breathe in a Christian subculture that does not always celebrate the gifting of women leaders.

During my doctoral studies I was graced with a research reflection team that was enthusiastic, thoughtful, helpful, and gracious. Dr. Jossie Owens, Dr. Jan Lanham, Dr. Nancy Ross, Dr. Marylou Shea, and Ms. Ruthanne Smith Mann have flooded me with prayerful encouragement. To be surrounded by such a circle of women is a gift beyond measure.

I give thanks for the many leaders, both male and female, from whom I have learned and continue to learn. Women in my study group, support group, and mentoring group have been especially pivotal; so a deep thanks to Vera, Laura, Katherine, Tami, Jossie, Margaret, Brenda, Claire, Kaza, Christy, and Mellissa for letting me into your lives, leadership struggles, and triumphs.

Thanks to my parents, Andy and Ann Rearick, who have always believed in me, and thanks to my mother-in-law, Judi Paul, for all her support. Thanks to the St. Paul's Church of the Nazarene, Olivet Nazarene University, and Point Loma Nazarene University with whom I have served as different portions of this book were written.

Most of all, I give thanks to God, in whom I live and breathe and have my being.

Now to [God] who by the power at work within us is able to accomplish abundantly far more than all we can ask or imagine, to him be glory in the church and in Christ Jesus to all generations, forever and ever. Amen.—*Ephesians 3:20-21*

# INTRODUCTION

*He [Jesus] took her by the hand and said to her, "Talitha cum,"*
*which means, "Little girl, get up!"*
—Mark 5:41

❧❧❧❧

❧ "Little girl, get up!" is a resurrection call and a command to all Christ followers. What a powerful message of new life these words carry as they are heard in all the dead places and spaces of our lives! *Talitha cum* is one of the few Aramaic phrases in the New Testament. This is striking, as it speaks to a strong memory recall of someone, or several people, who were present in this miraculous moment. These words were heard and etched into their memories. I picture the early disciples receiving these words of promise not just for this little girl but also as a broad assurance to all. The memory underlined by the use of the Aramaic quote speaks to the power of the voice of Jesus, which resonated as He spoke them. The echo of these memorable words reverberated over the challenges of their lives as they unfolded in surprising ways after the death and resurrection of Jesus Christ.

I have read this verse many times over the years. Growing up in church, I heard sermons on this text celebrating the power of Christ in the healing stories of the hemorrhaging woman and the raising of the daughter of Jairus as found in the gospel of Mark. It wasn't until seminary that I moved into a deeper experience with this passage. The discovery that there was something intentional being expressed by the sandwiching of the story of the hemorrhaging women into the story of Jairus's daughter opened up a new understanding of the depths of the healing being offered to both women. The implications of these healings and the call to a life of resurrection for people today have profound meaning.

This passage reached out and grabbed my attention again on an afternoon of meditation as this book began to take shape. After years of leading local congregations and talking with other women in leadership inside and outside the church walls, I heard this passage as a deep call of God. This double-healing story speaks a word of hope to all who suffer; it also has a particularly powerful message for women gifted and called to leadership but restrained by theological and sociological constructs.

There are also many suffering daughters, and even dying daughters, who are in the midst of our church communities. The call to "get up" is a command that resonated with my soul and moved from particular to personal to universal with a sense of weight and freedom. The richness of this story serves as the biblical foundation for the themes of the following pages.

"Little girl, get up" is clarion call to all women in the Christian community. Unlike many political movements, Jesus is not merely reshuffling the deck of power. It is the deep call of God with the good news of the resurrection to all women who have been bleeding out like the hemorrhaging woman, with no place to go, as well as those who are slowly dying in a limiting state of privilege like Jairus's daughter. It is an invitation to hear and obey God's deep reality-shifting message to all people—women and men, insiders and outsiders—to live out fully the life God has given us, gifted us for, and called us to live.

Some of us deny this call because of our fears. What will this kind of strength look like and feel like? Will I lose my femininity? Do I want to carry the weight and responsibility of the leadership potential God has given me?

Sometimes the call of God to resurrection is a call to rise up and attend to the tasks we have been given. Sometimes the call is to rise up into the fully reconciled relationship of love with our God. Sometimes the call is to rise up and embrace the potential of the gifts and graces given us. All of us are called to be disciples of Christ and receive the breadth of God's promises for His followers. This means we all have opportunity to speak, to learn, and to serve a church, an organization, a people, and ultimately God.

Sometimes the call is garbled because the community of faith can be quick to limit how a woman is to understand her potential role in the Church and in life. I still remember the crestfallen look of one of my early mentors when I described my call to pastoral ministry. While he wanted me to be a fully devoted follower of Christ, he assumed this would be expressed in submissive roles in my home, church, and work. The community of God is not always prepared to celebrate the call of resurrection in the life of the women of the Church.

And yet the call to resurrection is a persistent and powerful message of hope to all God's people. The typical journey of most women in leadership has been to seek *other* forms of service and work. It is only in the ongoing work of God that they have heard a strengthening call to rise up to the true purpose for which they were born. For some, the early beckoning of God can be seen in childhood play. Many of us had dolls we nurtured and cared for. We fed them and dressed them like our mothers dressed us. But we also lined them up and called them as congregations to repentance. Or we lined them up and began to teach them their school lessons. Or we lined them up and began to lead them to some imagined goal. Imaginative play frees a child to explore possibilities without the restraints of cultural limitations.

My own development as a pastoral leader has been formed by the Church, childhood play, important role models, and divinely opened doors. While there have been both inward and outward obstacles to naming God's call and fulfilling that call, I continue to hear Jesus calling me to arise when new opportunities arise. I am by nature a nest-builder, content and deeply relational. These things are great gifts in my life. They also make any of the changes and moves I have made deeply painful.

Nonetheless, I hear the whisper of God when I want to pull up the covers and stay in my soft bed a little longer: *Talitha cum.* In the name of Jesus, I arise. I pray for strength and begin walking about like the daughter of Jairus. In Mark's telling of the story, those who watch and hear Jesus' words are amazed. Amazement leads to a whole continuum of reactions from celebration to fearful anger. When Jesus takes us by the hand and says, *Talitha cum,* there is amazement and a whole array of reactions.

While my story is intertwined in the chapters of this book, I hope to engage us in a larger exploration. This book is not a defense of the women's call to leadership in church or in the workplace. That task is left to other able authors. Nor do I claim the themes of this book to be exclusively feminine. The issues and concerns regarding expected and accepted leadership qualities are experienced by men as well. On the contrary, I would propose that women experience these challenges in a broader and more layered manner that most men.

The purpose of this book is threefold. One is to explore the call of God on women to places of leadership. Another is to investigate internal and external obstacles to that call while uncovering certain myths often unspoken about women in leadership. Last, it is a celebration of God's amazing call, which hopefully serves as an encouragement to all God's people to rise up and walk.

# ONE

# A STORY OF HOPE FOR ALL

*Immediately the girl got up and began to walk about (she was twelve years of age). At this they were overcome with amazement.*

—Mark 5:42

❧❧❧

❧ Two biblical women who were receivers of Christ's resurrection hope are found in the Gospel of Mark. Both are nameless and referred to by disease or family relation. Yet they are remembered for their faith and resurrection. The healing stories found in Mark 5 are great individual narratives of a bleeding woman and the daughter of Jairus. In addition, these stories have profound implication for all people and in a deeply powerful way for women.

Ched Meyer's book *Binding the Strong Man* reveals the socio-cultural dynamics inherent in the coupling of the healing of Jairus's daughter and the woman with the blood flow.[1] Meyer's work opened my eyes to the importance of reading this passage as one story with authorial intentions regarding tensions, symbolisms, and commentary. A comparison of the two stories has clear implications for the powerless (hemorrhaging women) and the powerful (Jairus and by relation his daughter).

The indirect request by touch through the outstretched hand of a woman who was accustomed to being denied is dramatically contrasted with the direct request of Jairus, who was accustomed to asking and receiving favors. The bleeding woman reaches out from behind Jesus, indicating some sense of her worth and some sense of her desire to remain anonymous. Jairus meanwhile approaches Jesus directly while bowing before Him. His entrance still speaks about his sense of standing in the community and personal self-worth.

Another contrast is found when we note that Jairus calls out to Jesus to heal his daughter, indicating his love as a father and intimate connection. On the way to Jairus's home, Jesus stops, and after healing the unnamed bleeding woman, He calls her *daughter*. This woman who had no known family and no apparent commitment of love received words (overheard by her community) that indicated God's love and intimate connection.

These comparisons are heightened by the drama of the long pause taken between the request of the powerful and the attention given to the powerless. All of this has much to say to us about who needs resurrection (actually the poor and the rich) and who is included in the good news of Jesus Christ (all of us). There is also a clear statement being made about the judgments we often make about who is worthy of our attention and who is not. This is a particular struggle for those who have come from privilege and power. While I will speak to the challenges women in leadership face in society, I must never forget that I, too, have been formed by values that are not reflective of God's kingdom and must be shed.

The conviction of this passage continues to challenge me as I recognize how often I shut out or devalue my own version of the rejected bleeding woman or ways I can adopt limited expectations for myself or others. It has been heartening in a variety of settings to ask people to serve as biblical detectives and think about what is common between the two stories, what is distinct, what connects to other things we have read in the Scriptures, and what the implications might be for personal application.

There are, of course, some pieces of information that can quickly be named by the students. They note the common number twelve. Twelve years of bleeding, twelve years of age, twelve disciples, twelve tribes of Israel. With some digging they note the reference of Christ to the bleeding woman as *daughter* and the other healing being the *daughter* of Jairus.

They also comment on the parallel rising of the women. One is raised from her knees (unworthiness) the other is raised from her death bed (a death bed of relative luxury). As they continue the discussion they notice the comparison of a woman who has nothing to a young girl who seemingly has everything, but as we press in to the passage, several things can be seen to happen. One is that the students begin to see that stories they may consider known and familiar have exciting new aspects for them to discover. They also see themselves as capable of using their good minds to do the work of biblical interpretation.

Additionally, some of the female students begin to grapple with what this story has to say about how Jesus values women, calls them to life, and moves them from the fringe of society and the religious community into the very center of these groups. Jesus makes clear that while society may continue to push women to the fringes, they have a central place in God's unfolding kingdom, which has come and is coming through Jesus himself.

Mark reveals Jesus as the catalyst for the coming of God's kingdom. This kingdom invites those who have been outcast and disenfranchised to a new understanding of themselves as valued and belonging. The values of God's kingdom include honoring, loving, and raising up daughters of God. The power of Christ brings healing and restoration to community of those who have been shut out.[2] These women both embodied the very definition of *unclean*. One was continuously bleeding, the other a corpse.[3] Jesus' affirmation of one woman's touch and His reaching out to the other marks His ministry as a counter-cultural movement.

While we may need reminding of just how unexpected Jesus' actions were, those in power at the time were certainly taking notice. Jesus' stubborn ministry to the fringe members of society gave rise to increasing conflict with the authorities. This building conflict ultimately led Him to Jerusalem. The resurrection that is offered to us is founded in Jesus' loving sacrifice, which calls all to belonging in the kingdom of God.

These are important words for women in leadership to hear. When we are not heard by others, God hears our voices. When our work is not recognized, or is diminished or denied, God celebrates our obedience. One colleague shared her frustration during staff meetings. She would offer a suggestion for a new program idea, and initially it would be ignored or dismissed. But when a male staff member would pick up the idea, it would be affirmed—most often without acknowledgement that she was the original source. While she needed to find a way to name the experience to her supervisor, she did find comfort that the many good ideas were implemented and that ultimately God knew and valued her contribution.

When others tell us that our leadership is inappropriate, un-biblical, and destructive to the family, our affirmation from God remains. When one of my friends was in the midst of breaking through a barrier in our denominational leadership system, there was much debate. Among strong supporters, there were also those who questioned her abilities and even her "right" to the position.

During this time of transition she had a dream in which she was driving along the turnpike when a state trooper pulled her over. He checked her license and vehicle registration and called in for her driving record. Her anxiety built while she waited for him to return. Finally he came back and with a look of disbelief across his face handed her back the license and registration. He said that she checked out, was legitimate, and then he waved her on her way. From there she traveled through different environments; desert, forest, and finally a city that she had never been in before.

There she met a man who walked and talked with her for miles and miles. When she looked into His face, she could not determine His features but saw that His eyes were ageless and had wisdom beyond comprehension. She knew even in the midst of her dream that it was the Lord. Upon waking, she sensed God speaking into her heart that she was His legitimate choice for this position and was not to allow the questions and doubts of others to dissuade her. She also knew that God had promised to be with her on the journey.

Over the years I have met many women who, upon responding to God's call, were told by family, church, and others that they must have heard wrong. Even more difficult was when people close to them insisted that not only were they hearing wrong but also that their very testimonies were an aberration to God. Thankfully, God kept speaking and calling them to live out their life's call. Often God provided key people who interrupted the shaming language of others. These people who prayed with them, who offered wise counsel, affirmation, and hope, were vital to the renewal of their call.

God invites the desperate to call out for wholeness beyond physical healing. When Jesus says to the hemorrhaging woman, "Your faith has saved you,"[4] He affirms her larger desperation. Her pain, though certainly physical, was also emotional, spiritual, and psychological. However, out of such desperation was born a fearlessness that bore the fruit of salvation for this woman. She initiated this encounter. She reached out for healing uninvited. All the resources of this world had failed her, but she was sure that if she could just touch Jesus' clothes, a miracle could happen.

Out of her reckless act a healing power poured out of Jesus and changed her life. It is interesting to note that when Jesus asked, "Who touched me?" His words made clear that this healing was not some magical happenstance because someone simply bumped into Him. At the moment of her touching Him a large crowd was already penning in on Him. Many people inadvertently touched Him. It was the particular touch of a person of faith—however desperate—that was distinctly healing and salvific. Fear could have kept this bleeding woman captive, but desperation moved her beyond that fear to an act of faith.

Desperation is never a comfortable place for any of us to reach. And yet it is in this place that we can be open to the work of God in new ways. In the Evangelical tradition we celebrate the wonderful testimonies of people who were desperate due to addictions, empty pursuits, relational brokenness, and personal distress. However, when this desperation is not born of personal sin but rather the frustration of gender limitations, there is little if any celebration. Instead, the common reaction can be a bit like the utter befuddlement of the disciples in the story when they could not figure out why Jesus would stop to look for the one who touched Him.

When the news of the twelve-year-old girl's death reached Jesus and Jairus, Jesus responded, "Do not fear, only believe" (Mark 5:36). He was again making an important connection to belief in God's saving ways through Jesus. The breakthrough for many women has been found when male members of the system see their own daughters' pain because of limitations that have been set forth. I have heard some refer to changes made in church polity to include women in leadership "the daughter clause." It is in the close range of loving relationships that we often are willing to make room for some group we would otherwise have shut out. Jairus might not have cared much for the issues of resurrection for all women, but he knew he was willing to call upon Jesus on behalf of the one he loved, his daughter.

Fear is often the enemy for women called into areas of leadership. It can hold women captive who have gifts and graces that are desperately needed in our world and our churches. Fear without action can be a jail, a place where a woman can know that something is wrong about the way she is living but is unable or unwilling to envision any other possibility than being stuck in the current situation. Some women discover new wholeness out of desperation when their circumstances or inner chaos leads them to believe they will die if they do not reach out by faith and ask God to fulfill His resurrection promise in and through their lives. Like the bleeding woman, they often don't know what the ramifications of the power of Jesus will bring in their lives, but they know "If I but touch him I will be healed." And they dare to reach out for the wholeness that stops the bleeding and reinstates them to a place of value and belonging.

Sometimes I call the origins of this holy desperation a *holy discontent*. This is a discontent regarding life's present situation. Again, this is not a story of a rebellious child like the prodigal found in Luke 15, who wakes up to his situation and heads home. It is the story of the daughter of a rich leader who has been lulled to sleep with comforts that can cover the deeper need to know the resurrection life in its fullness. Yet she begins to push back the comforts, recognizing that she is called to more than this. This stirring of the Holy Spirit can be disconcerting. It is the kind of stirring that messes up a lot of people's plans.

When a woman begins to discover gifts for leadership and a calling to use those gifts in various settings, the family systems can become very unsettled. This discomfort often increases as the woman's role expands in her workplace and can make new demands on her immediate family. The initial conversations with husbands who had generally been supportive found this new vision for their shared future disconcerting. These men had not envisioned their wives living life this way, and they knew it would demand some changes in their plans. This demands patience, forgiveness, and prayer on the part of both spouses. Personal growth in a marriage demands flexibility from both partners.

Larger family systems will struggle with these changes as well. Families who have had a traditional mind-set that women were primarily support systems for the men to flourish struggle with a new paradigm where the husband may make personal and professional sacrifices for the woman to flourish.

Family systems may be more understanding of a cross-country move for a man's career as opposed to a woman's career. Stories around tables of women with leadership careers refer to family members who roll their eyes when the women assert themselves or poke at them with words like "Aren't you full of yourself?" when they talk about their work.

This leadership growth has added anxiety for family systems when the woman refers to a call to pastoral leadership. Not only did the family not see the daughter, sister, or wife as a leader, but they also had never envisioned any woman as a pastor. One friend reported a conversation with her husband, who initially could not imagine sitting under a woman's preaching for his spiritual care, let alone his wife's preaching. Another friend talked about her mother's insistence on recognizing her husband's call and ordination while ignoring her daugher's. Ultimately family systems can be quite content with how things have always been. A woman's growth and change in the system can be disconcerting and quite virulently resisted. Systems do not always celebrate the resurrection life of its members.

As with many new ideas or ways of being, it can feel very uncomfortable, and the discomfort can sometimes be interpreted as a sign that it is wrong. In the Christian community we have often used *internal peace* as the ultimate litmus test. Peace and a sense of rightness are eventually important to our discernment process, but it is a faulty primary indicator of life direction. We can feel peace because of ignorance or become quite unsettled because God is doing something new. A woman who is called to live out her gifts and strengths in leadership must be obedient to that call. The distress it may cause for others is secondary to obedience. Clearly it is vital to allow space for significant others to pray, adjust to new futures, and discern with the one called to new leadership roles. It is also important that the journey in marriage is not about only one member exercising his or her gifts. Many women and men are learning to hear new ways God is calling their spouses to live out their resurrection lives.

Holy desperation, holy discontent, and holy callings make new ways for us to reach out to touch the hem of Christ's robe. These same stirrings also serve as important impetus for people to reach out to God on behalf of those they love. In response to these outstretched prayers the healing ministry of Christ flows in places we were not even aware were broken. This woman knew she needed the blood to stop flowing, but she may not have realized how much she needed Jesus to call her out before the community and affirm her as *daughter*. Jairus knew his daughter needed a healing touch as she laid her weary head down for the last time, but he may not have realized how much she needed Jesus to call her out of her comfortable home to new life.

I love to hear my friends talk during those times of stirring. Each journey is distinct yet similar. There is a beautiful sense that God is taking them to new places, and in those times it is important to recall the words of Jesus: "Don't be afraid; just believe" (Mark 5:36, NIV). Often they will begin some sort of educational process and name where it will *not* lead. They offer limiting comments such as "I am taking this course to help me lead small groups, but I'm not going to be a pastor" or "I am getting education to be a better counselor but only for part time work" or "I am developing this new skill just for this project, not so it will become a profession." I think these kinds of statements are often an unconscious shield against the eventual life change that deep in their hearts they know is coming. And yet the simple act of obedience to what we can see of God's call opens all of us up to new directions and larger changes than we could have imagined.

Some women receive healing as they reach out in desperation. Yet others receive it when the touch of God seems to wake them from a deep sleep. The daughter of Jairus is a passive character due to illness. In her dormant state she represents many of us who fall asleep in this life, allowing parts of ourselves to become dead. There is great symbolism for budding life when we think of all that is happening in a twelve-year-old girl.[5] The daughter of Jairus would have been considered at the age of marriage and therefore a potential source of life in marriage and children. This potential for life has an important parallel to many women called to move beyond their limited understanding of themselves and other women. So many have impending possibilities to be the source of life when their gifts and talents are fully offered to God and they are given space to flourish.

The loss when a woman is not able to live out the fullness of her calling and life is not just personal. There is community growth and fruitfulness that is lost as well. In my own church the percentage of women given ministry leadership opportunities in the church dropped from a high of approximately twenty-five percent to a low of one percent.[6] When one recognizes the results of a sociological shift of an institution that once encouraged women to one that has restrained women, there is grief over the evident loss.

It is important to mourn not only the personal stories of restriction but mourn as well the churches, missions, and compassionate ministries that may have been born or grown had the women called during those times been given opportunities to serve. Florence Nightingale spoke of similar realities in her church experience: "I would have given her [the church] my head, my heart, my hand. She would not have them. . . . She told me to go back and do crochet in my mother's drawing room."[7]

Women continue to voice this frustration. In 1853 Phoebe Palmer, a Holiness evangelist called the Church "a sort of potter's field, where the gifts of women, as so many strangers, are buried."[8] She went on to pray, "O Lord, how long before man shall roll away the stone that we may see a resurrection?"[9]

I regularly hear women talk about their frustration regarding their personal and professional growth that is not recognized or valued by their local churches. They feel as if there is so much they could offer that is largely ignored.

There is holy discontentment, and there is unholy content-ment. At times we are quite settled in our understanding of who God is and who we are in relation to God and others, but a restrained vision for God and ourselves causes us to miss out on the adventure of fully following Christ. Life devolves into surviving but not really living. This is not the life Christ came to bring to all who follow Him. This is not the abundant life Jesus proclaimed. As people who are living in cooperation with the Holy Spirit, joining in the divine work of God every day, we know there is no such thing as status quo. But we some-times settle for something less, because it is so easy to settle for comforting levels of safety. Yet at some point, if we are left to limited visions for our lives, we can become increasingly angry, depressed, or bored. This can create great unfocused angst in a Christian woman's life. She might struggle over the limitations and wonder if this safe place she has lived is the best place to live after all.

I have seen these different emotions expressed by women in the Church. Pastors sometimes call them "church bosses." They become protective of the little they can claim as their own, whether that is a particular church program, the color of a Sunday School classroom, or even the role definition that has hemmed them in. They are ready to fight over little things be-cause they have already lost so much. The alternative to this anger is a boredom that causes them to walk away from their church. Either way, they miss out on the fullness of the res-urrection life offered through Jesus Christ. Thankfully, Jesus keeps entering, showing up in our place of deadness, and takes us by the hand, calling us to rise up. If we respond to God's commands, amazing miracles can happen. This call might not be to a leadership position, but it's always a call to be more and share more in the life-giving work of God in our world. The ris-ing up of the daughter of Jairus is a call for all of us who have fallen asleep to the point of death to open our eyes, to awaken. Rise up, daughter. There is more for you to do.

# TWO

# DEEPER RESURRECTION

*I want to know Christ and the power of his resurrection and the fellowship of sharing in his sufferings, becoming like him in his death, and so, somehow, to attain to the resurrection from the dead.*
—Philippians 3:10-11, NIV

❧❧❧

❧ The words of Jesus *Talitha cum* call all of us to a full resurrection. Yet resurrection comes with a cost; we must actually rise up and live. Ruts—unhealthy or unfulfilling routines and limitations—can be signs of a person choosing less than the abundant life promised to those who are disciples of Christ. Many of us can find a strange but familiar comfort in situations that have frustrations and tensions yet are known experiences rather than unknown horizons. There can be a nominal happiness in a wealthier community that comes with consumption, false sense of progress, and achievement. Satisfaction with the status quo can be quite a lulling experience. Yet, as Paul expresses in Philippians, I do want to know the fullness of the power of the resurrection at work within me.

In Philippians 3 Paul speaks powerfully of a full-hearted desire to know the resurrection of Christ at work in and through your life. Clearly this passage connects the power of the resurrection at work in us to a submission and obedience that will lead to death, metaphorically or literally. This message of submission has sometimes been interpreted as constraining and limiting, but it is actually quite freeing. If God is the ultimate authority in the guidance and direction of my life, the constraints of society have a looser hold. Dying to self often releases women who may have been constrained by social mores and/or the limited expectations of the Church to discover facets of their gifts and passions through a process of simple obedience to God's call. While I must show good work of discernment with consideration for the authority of scripture, the affirmation of my faith community, and an understanding of tradition, there is a place in which we speak of God's leading us in surprising ways.

Many women empowered by the work of God in their lives have taken positions of leadership and broken through barriers out of obedience to God. The early women preachers in the Holiness Movement did not consider themselves advocates of women's rights. Their primary concern was obedience to God's call.[1] The "sanctified self" offered freedom to explore God's will outside of gender restrictions. Their holy desire was to "know Christ and the power of his resurrection" (Philippians 3:10). To do anything less than preach, teach, start compassionate ministries, and invite neighbors to life in Christ was to live in disobedience to God's call and deny the resurrection they had received. Their journey was not one of claiming personal rights or an epiphany of women's issues. Their motivation was to be surrendered to God.

This primary motivation continues to be significant for Christian women who move into leadership positions today. This does not dismiss the important voices of women who have critiqued unjust systems both inside and outside the Church. In addition, the primary motivation of obedience does not demand silence from women when treatment is unfair or laden with issues of harassment.

I have found there is some confusion among Christian women regarding identification with the feminist movement. When feminism is defined in terms of valuing, caring, and providing space for women to flourish, there is general assent and agreement. Unfortunately there are other political, moral, and ideological constructs that many assume are included in the definition of *feminist*. This leads to confusion for many Christian women. Some create a complete separation between their feminist views of themselves as capable, valued professionals and what they both experience and embrace as restricted female roles in the Church. I have known women who are vocal in their insistence for fair treatment at work but continue serving in church fellowships that do not allow women to serve on leadership committees and certainly not as pastors. Other women simply reject feminism as foreign to their Christian faith. Others work hard to articulate a thoughtful explanation of what a person means by calling herself a Christian feminist.

This tension can lead to mixed messages. Some women have experienced the journey into leadership as one particular just for them and do not comprehend the real implications their journeys have for all women. The very woman who speaks to thousands will denounce a woman's right to preach. I remember my shock when I heard Elizabeth Elliot do this at a large session during a New England Evangelical Association meeting in Boston. Women can be given permission to engage in leadership tasks that are considered emergencies but are not allowed to lead in a so-called *normal* setting. I have heard women say they believed God's call came to them only because the men who were supposed to lead were not listening. I hear young women today who, while training for professions that will demand leadership, say women are "too emotional," "too unstable," or "too unpredictable" to be the leader in charge.

There are layers of difficulty with these messages. The most disturbing for me is the denial of a woman's creation in the image of God. What many female students describe is really the assumption that women never grow into full adulthood. These women do not imagine a future in which they might have independence or that their gifts and graces could extend to anything beyond a supporting role. Support roles are significant and important, but they are not gender-specific. I have witnessed many frustrated women who were born to be leaders but because of a false sense of limitation have remained in support roles. The frustration this creates can often demand they use back-door ways to exert their leadership.

As I participated in the ordination process for new candidates, several times the committee reflected on the call of a husband and wife. While the husband was presented as the candidate, the wisdom of the committee sensed it was the wife who had the gifts, graces, and real calling to ministry. It seemed these women were trying to fulfill their call to leadership through their husbands. We assessed this was not healthy for either partner.

This limitation by gender also expresses a failure to believe in the power of the resurrection for women. When the gospel invitation is given to enter new life in and through Christ, there is a subtext for many Christian women.

This subtext says, "As you listen to God, here are the preconceived limitations for who you can be, what jobs you can hold, and where you can go." This seems to be the opposite message of total submission to God. So rather than a full yes to God, it is a limited one. In addition, some teach submission in all of a woman's relationships that ultimately sets up male mediators between women and God. This again is not true to the biblical invitation to a reconciled relationship with God through Christ.

An implication of one woman's limited view is that other women are not called to know the fullness of God's Spirit by her testimony and model. Personal resurrection is always for the purpose of corporate resurrection. The problem is not only that women have not known the fullness of what God desired to do in their lives because of these limitations but also that the community of God suffered as well.

It is part of the tradition of many churches that testimonies are regularly given as a word of hope for all people. If the one who testifies says, "God filled me with His presence, and through His power I have been able to effectively lead," then how can we insist to others that because of gender this cannot be true in their lives?

Jesus said to Martha, "I am the resurrection and the life" (John 11:25), and a shift occurred. While He was responding to the death of Lazarus, clearly He was saying so much more. The promise is inclusive: "I am the resurrection and the life. Those who believe in me, even though they die, will live" (John 11:25). The good news of Christ's resurrection includes women. He continued with His proclamation of good news and asked Martha directly, "Do you believe this?" (John 11:26). If our answer is yes, we must let the fullness of this good news be received by all persons, both women and men.

At the same time, I must confess that at times I stumble over the necessity to share in His sufferings in becoming like Him in His death. When reading Paul's words in Philippians, I call out with great passion, "I want to know Christ and the power of His resurrection," but my voice gets much quieter if I continue with the verse and say "and the fellowship of sharing in His suffering." Like most North Americans, I do not embrace those uncomfortable notions easily.

Nevertheless I have found words like *suffering* and *death* to be essential realities when one truly leads. A group of Christian women leaders with whom I met on a monthly basis often discussed making peace with death. As leaders they knew the only way to effectively lead an organization through change was to lead without the tyranny of fear. Fear can grab hold of any leader. Fear of failure, the unknown, looking foolish or inept, conflict, and pain for self or others can constrain any of us into ineffective attempts at leadership. To lead is to engage in battle. We must lead while acknowledging those fears.

Courage is not fearlessness; it understands the potential harm and still boldly engages in the hard work of leadership. This is not the kind of battle in which you inflict your will and ways on others. It is the battle a parent faces when he or she raises a child, or a teacher has when he or she seeks to instruct a group of students. It is a battle for the future of those you love and serve.

Marva Dawn described this battle from a preacher's perspective this way: "We are painting a vision of the kingdom of God in opposition to the reign in this world of other powers, so it is a spiritual battle we are fighting, which will also physically exhaust us."[2]

When we are offering a countercultural vision, when we battle against gods whose glittering presence seeks to consume, or lolling sirens who offer temptations to sleep, we will be exhausted. There is a physical, emotional and spiritual cost to those battles. A person moving into true leadership must know that offering a vision-casting, prophetic, or awakening voice, even when it's with a deep desire to serve others, can illicit angry or anxiety-filled responses. This inevitably means the leader will be a target for the expressions of those emotions, and battle scars are the inevitable result.

My women friends all had battle scars from their struggles to fulfill God's call to leadership. It was tempting to withdraw from that which causes suffering and pain. And yet as we shared our stories, we discovered avoidance was not a real option. To fail to lead those we are called to love—families, churches, parachurch ministries, and people we serve through vocational commitments—would ultimately be a choice not to love them at all. We urged each other on and prayed for the wisdom and strength to love and to lead with boldness and love. This group was essential in helping me move beyond the temptation to stay in more comfortable places. They also offered me reassurance that my call to fulfill the leadership moment was important and significant for me and the community I served.

After our times of prayer together I found my wounds were blanched and my commitment to lead emboldened. I was on the right track. As I took the awkward and necessary first steps, they encouraged me to believe in what God was stirring in my soul, and they grieved with me when that sometimes meant taking the blows that come with true leadership.

All leaders, not just women, find suffering to be real and the willingness to die to ourselves a necessity. In Thom Rainer's book *Breakout Churches*[3] he states that he is hesitant to name a surprising discovery. He found a common experience among pastors who led churches in times of transition and change—all suffered deep wounds for their efforts. While each story was unique in its manifestation, they all experienced betrayal, misunderstanding, loss of friendships, and personal attacks.

Rainer sums it up with this statement: "The cost of following Christ is great. We cannot become complacent with the status quo just to avoid conflict."[4] His concern was that by stating the common leadership experience of suffering, some might pull back from leading their churches with boldness. As people lead, the organizations, churches or otherwise, have a way of letting a bold leader know that his or her changes, his or her vision, is threatening.

When people feel threatened, they find ways of fighting back. This fight can be overt or subversive, but it comes, and it hurts. The only way we continue in leadership is to have a higher vision than our personal comfort. This vision can be thwarted by things like ego, lust for power, or control. With all honesty, these characteristics can invade the motivations and passions of the leader as well as those who might fight the leader. Hopefully for us as Christians, the larger vision for which we are willing to sacrifice is one given to us by God and empowered by the Holy Spirit. The gift of my circle of women friends was their commitment not only to support me and encourage me in the leadership battles I faced but also to confront me when my reactions or attitudes were more about my ego than about my call. When the inevitable tensions arise, it is paramount that the leader is also able to reflect and review where his or her actions, inactions, words, or silence contributed to the discord. A Christian leader, whether fulfilling a vocation within or outside the church walls, is called to dependence upon the Holy Spirit for appropriate humility as well as boldness.

There have been several times when I have stepped into leadership and someone has remarked, "Aren't you full of yourself?" This statement would often set me on my heels a bit. While there may have been a few times when it was true, for the most part these were simply moments in which I was exuding confidence in the gifts God had given me and the presence of God within me. Leadership for a woman of God is not about being full of self, as some might charge. This leadership is born of being filled of the Spirit and walking according to the whispers of God. It is the difficult task of leaders to discern when the discordant voices are raising appropriate concerns and when they are not. Most women have been socialized to be peacemakers; therefore, the extra layer of burden for these leaders is not to give up out of personal anxiety when turbulent times occur. To be confident in our calling and in our God is not a commitment to lose Christlike service to others.

The battle scars from leadership give rise to the ongoing need for God to heal and restore us in times of battle. In the same women's group where we discussed our need to "make peace with death," we also discussed the necessity of being tough-skinned and soft-hearted. We discovered it was very easy as leaders to lose our way as we lead. If we did not remain prayerful and grace-filled, we could become bitter and hardened as we dealt with blows from the very people we hoped to serve. If our hearts were allowed to become hardened, we knew from experience that the brittle edges might protect us from being hurt, but they would also lessen our ability to hear God speak into our hearts. If we continued in that state, it would eventually affect all our relationships.

As the group as a whole did, I found that a hardened heart caused times of corporate worship to feel empty, that I was on edge, and that my frustrations with life increased. When my heart was hardened it gave me a false sense that I was building strength as I developed brittle attitudes, and that I dismissed the opinions of others and charged ahead in the direction I assumed to be correct. Yet I lost so much along the way. I lost the wonder of life, the awe of God's new words of direction, the connection to God, others, and self.

As other members of this group experienced these same challenges, we were each tempted to pull away either physically or psychologically from the honest voices offering accountability and support. Thankfully, we fought to keep each other from remaining isolated, and we prayed for each other and watched as the work of the Holy Spirit melted our hearts. We each had testimonies of times when we were driving to this or that task and were suddenly overwhelmed with God's presence, singing in church and immersed in God's love, or awakened in the middle of the night by the presence of the Holy Spirit calling us to forgive, to love, to be merciful, and to receive forgiveness.

The Lord's Prayer reminds us that forgiveness is a daily call. It is the essential work of every Christian to learn to receive and extend forgiveness. The Christian leader is in a place where this essential work has especially intense seasons. This work of forgiveness demands discernment regarding when to take action, when to confront, and when to let go. In ongoing situations we also must determine when it is necessary to create protective boundaries from the hurtful actions of others. This journey is difficult and cannot be lived perfectly. It is the messy work of all our lives.

It was in one of those particularly difficult leadership times I remembered a practice I learned from a spiritual formation book.[5] The authors offered the practice of taking the Lord's Prayer and inserting someone's name as a way of praying for that person. I certainly do this with people I love, but I have found it to be an important practice in praying for those with whom I have unresolved tensions. It stretched my prayers to remember this person as more than our disagreement. The prayer also calls me to pray forgiveness even when I am not feeling the desire in any way.

When I called out to God, "Forgive Joe his trespasses as he forgives the trespasses of others,"[6] an important shift occurred in my soul. I was not praying that *Joe* would come to know the error of his ways, which is my propensity. Nor was I praying for the fulfillment of some dream sequence in which Joe apologizes and announces to the whole community how wrong he has been. I was praying that Joe would know mercy and extend mercy, and in that prayer was the underlying desire that Joe would flourish.

The strength to lead is grounded in our spiritual walk, but there is the need for all of us to learn skills and insights from other leaders. Many leadership books can teach us, yet we may experience limitations when we try to apply those lessons to our own leadership styles.

One issue for women is that most of the books, conferences, and trainings have been written or led by men. I have learned much from many of these men, yet often personal re-contextualization was needed. This work was greatly enhanced when I gathered with other women. In those settings we shared content and leadership teaching that we connected with and information that created dissonance. I discovered new breath in my vocation as we shared common leadership challenges and the particular ways women responded to those challenges.

In these groups I heard other women grieve broken relationships when those they loved did not understand their decisions. I also learned that not everybody I work alongside of needs to be my friend. This sounds strange as I write it, and maybe it is a particular notion that women can carry in our leadership. Many of us want all our relationships to be harmonious and even intimate. In leadership you discover this is not a possibility. Leadership demands difficult and sometimes controversial decisions. This can cause a loss of intimacy as those who work under your authority may be disappointed and carry

that disregard into the relationship. There are natural personality conflicts that arise due to our different strengths, ways of
being, and even our roles within an institution. Leadership can
be a lonely experience.

Sometimes those we work with are damaged by past experiences and have been hurt in ways that prevent them from
working with us in a healthy manner. The challenge is being
able to discern if working through the difficulties with the person is positive for the organization as a whole or if it is time
to part ways. The leader's decision is often second-guessed in
such a situation. A leader may make the decision to part ways
with the best of intentions, take all the right actions, approach
the situation with a loving heart, and still be perceived by others as harsh, mean, and controlling. This misconception is often fueled because the leader is restricted by what he or she can
say and how much of the complete story can be shared. Leaders
must be willing to be misunderstood.

Christian power ultimately demands suffering, because
the resurrection power is always in service of others, not self.
The ongoing rhythm of Christian leaders is connecting and
reconnecting with God in spiritual practices that renew, fill,
refresh, and heal, then pouring themselves out once again.
So prayerfully, and perhaps with some trepidation, I want to
know Christ and the power of His resurrection and the fellowship of sharing in His sufferings, in optimistic faith that
this will be the venue for all of us to know the resurrection
from the dead.

# THREE

# WE NEED WOMEN LEADERS

*We have gifts that differ according to the grace given to us; prophecy,*
*in proportion to faith; ministry, in ministering; the teacher, in teaching;*
*the exhorter, in exhortation; the giver; in generosity; the leader,*
*in diligence; the compassionate, in cheerfulness.*
—Romans 12:6-8

❧ The ultimate benefit of releasing women to new leadership roles is not simply to allow some particular women to flourish. The leadership of gifted women is a benefit to the larger society. In various contexts—business, education, healthcare, and the Church—there have been expressed yearnings for new leadership to arise. All of that is available if women are willing and are given space to grow into that leadership.

In the recent studies of women in leadership, the findings suggest the distinctive contributions in thought and action that arose from women are not missing in male leadership but are not dominant characteristics or themes that arise when only men are in leadership positions.[1] The presence of the female voice at the table will allow some latent values rise to a more significant level. During decision-making discussions a woman may name concerns or a possible goal that is not adverse to the men's values and yet would not have been addressed without women being present. Women often have eyes and ears that see and hear sometimes subtle implications of decisions that are sometimes missed by the men on the leadership teams.

I had the privilege of serving with two other women on a board that had previously been all-male. One of the tasks of this board was to serve as gatekeepers for those returning to ordained ministry after a season away either by choice or by discipline. We had one candidate whose situation was presented. There was an opportunity to meet with the candidate, and we discussed what led to his leaving his ministry and why he felt ready to return. After the candidate had left the room the board entered into the process of making a decision. Initially various men in the group presented their support of the candidate's return to ministry. The women members voiced some concerns. Each had significant objections regarding the way the candidate presented the situation, talked about women in his life, and expressed isues with responsibility and blame. This would not have been heard or voiced without women being present on that board.

Women are also willing to fight for issues that may concern men but would not become a primary focus of their work. Sue Thomas talks about this in the political arena:

> Women in office do indeed make distinctive contributions that transcend their symbolic function of diversifying politics. Perhaps the most dramatic of their contributions has been the distinctive policy priorities women elective and appointive officeholders have pursued. Women have concentrated, far more than men, on issues of women, children, and family . . . [and] have achieved passage of legislation in these areas at a greater rate than men.[2]

For legislation to pass, men had to vote to support the bill, yet without the women making this legislation a priority it would not have happened. These programs and policies were not adverse to the values of the men; they simply were not a focus until the women raised the issues.

Women in leadership offer new problem-solving approaches to some old constraints and issues. Creative dynamics are discovered when new people are brought to the tables of power. The result of creating healthy forms of diverse thinking and decision-making will ultimately serve the organization well.

This increase in creativity was evident in the life of the Shakers. Despite the fact that they were a small group, their inventions were numerous, such as seed catalogs, flat brooms, clothes pins, and the process for making evaporated milk.[3] One possible reason for this creativity was the way they rotated men and women into different tasks and gained new perspectives. Thomas R. Hawkins offers this perspective:

> Because they rotated across traditional gender categories and functional areas, people could look at tasks and roles without the limitations imposed by the culturally determined mental models into which they had been socialized.[4]

Sometimes people have defended women in leadership by writing essays about how the world, the Church, or the city would be different if women were in charge. This raises the ongoing debate regarding gender identity as essentialist or constructivist. Are women essentially more nurturing, relational, peace-seeking than men? In many ways we cannot answer this question without a long study over generations to discover if women's ways of being, knowing, and learning changed as gender roles changed.

I do know that the assumption that women leaders will by nature create a serving, loving, nurturing world is a false one. This is not the answer that is healthy for any of us. Women are not without issues of power, domination, or violence. Neither are men without kindness, compassion, or commitment. We hurt ourselves by swinging with pendulums. It is the call of the Garden of Eden that we might actually be partners in all aspects of this life together.

Joesph Coleson in his work on the first two chapters of Genesis establishes a biblical foundation for this call to partnership. The partnership pictured in the Creation account exhibits Adam and Eve valuing each other and understanding that each is made in the image of God. The creation of the human pair is not as one as the designated helper to the designated leader. Instead, a much more beautiful picture of gender mutuality emerges. Genesis 2:18 states, "I will make for it an "ezer cenegdo."[5] This is often translated as a "subservient helper." Women have been told their role is to help the men fulfill their leadership role. Yet when this word is used in other contexts, it has a much different meaning. Coleson notes, "When the Bible speaks of a helper, it usually refers to God the Helper, the Rescuer of those who cannot help themselves."[6] The creation account therefore presents us a picture of man and woman created to serve God together. They, like the Trinitarian God, have a community within which they can thrive and flourish. Coleson goes on to say, "God did it this way so human beings would understand that human companionship, especially between man and woman, is a priceless gift from God."[7]

I have found this companionship a priceless gift in the context of my marriage. Yet I think that this gift is not limited to marriage. This is the order God intended for all our cross-gender relationships. This is the order God intended in our workplaces, our homes, and our churches. Ruth Barton, working with this same passage from Genesis, concluded, "The male-female team that God created was not characterized by hierarchical authority structures but by an equal sharing of power, strength, and helpfulness."[8] This is not a call to special rights for women; rather, it is an invitation into a mutually supportive team that empowers every person to serve God and others in world transforming ways.

One step into this mutuality is to express and enact the valuing of men and women. It is startling when we pull back from conversations how many of our comments, often with attempts at humor, reflect something less. In offhanded comments made from pulpits, in women's and men's gatherings, both in professional and nonprofessional settings, we can be quite dismissive regarding the ways and actions of the opposite sex. It takes real work to move into a true respect and value of those we find different from ourselves. This work includes sometimes voicing concerns and sometimes silencing our own tongues from flippant remarks. We must be both prophetic and confessional.

For mutuality in relationship to occur, old ways of being have to change, and that can be difficult for those who are quite comfortable with the status quo. This discomfort is for men who have established ways of working with male colleagues and functioning in the atmosphere of a particular kind of workplace. This discomfort is also for women who find positions of power a novel and even awkward experience. Shifts in leadership teams will put all people on a learning curve.

One friend of mine expressed his surprise at the amount of emotional distress some new women staff members brought to their staff meetings. He was completely baffled by the shedding of tears and expressions of hurt during these gatherings. This was not something he wanted to handle in the workplace. The uncomfortable meetings were indicators that as the leader he might need to explore some new approaches to decision-making and collaboration. These meetings were also a signal that these women might need to find new ways of expressing concerns and entering into leadership challenges.

The work to truly enter into mutually empowered relationships has the potential for kingdom-building outcomes. When women and men are free to fulfill God's call beyond gender expectations, there is an opportunity for all people to flourish. Where people are flourishing, there is joy. Where there is joy, there are contagious expressions of God's kingdom.

We are not without biblical examples. Before the Fall, Adam and Eve had a cooperative relationship caring for the garden (see Genesis). Deborah was able to offer her gifts as a leader to her community (see Judges). Priscilla and Aquila were an effective ministry team (see Acts). A list of men and women in Paul's greetings found in Romans 16 affirms gifts and graces regardless of gender. All these examples fulfill the description in Romans 12:

As in one body we have many members, and not all the members have the same function, so we, who are many, are one body in Christ, and individually we are members one of another. We have gifts that differ according to the grace given to us: prophecy, in proportion to faith; ministry, in ministering; the teacher; in teaching; the exhorter, in exhortation; the giver; in generosity; the leader, in diligence; the compassionate, in cheerfulness *(Romans 12:4-8).*

This passage does not explore a gender basis for roles but rather a gift basis. This allows every member of the community the opportunity to grow and flourish to the glory of God. If we truly embraced this celebration of community, we would not be evaluating each other on the jobs we have or the titles we hold. We would simply be asking, "How are you living out God's call and gifting in your life?"

It is to the detriment of the Christian community (if not a definition of sin) when anyone is unable by systemic obstacles or unwilling by personal resistance to fulfill his or her life vocation. I have heard men questioned about their motives when they have been called to a teaching ministry at a daycare center. I have heard women questioned about their commitment to their children when they express a gifting for leadership. I have heard men who work under the leadership of a woman questioned about their "weakness." I have seen women with authority referred to as masculine.

These kinds of comments reflect the great discomfort when people move out of stereotypical roles. Part of the discomfort comes from having to stretch ourselves into relating to each new person without preconceived boxes. If men and women are given the freedom to serve each other and serve God as He gifts us, then we are free to enter into a new kind of relationship with one another. This true friendship can gloriously invade our marriages and our relationships across gender lines.

Failing to receive and celebrate another is to mark him or her as "other" and not our neighbor. We each have a call to love and to care for each person we encounter. One of the obstacles for men and women working in partnership are the concerns regarding sexual temptation. In reaction to the sexual indiscretions of some, there has been a rather significant reaction in the Evangelical world to create strong boundaries between women and men. Rather than these helping us in our relationships, we actually have built impenetrable walls that mark the other (man or woman) as a stranger in our midst. While we need to recognize our sexuality and potential temptations, it is important that we not build "hedges" of protection that allow significant cross-gender relationships with only spouses or family members. Some of these personal policies make working with the opposite sex so difficult that the natural outcome is a gender bias in hiring. This is especially true of smaller organizations. The thought is *If I can't be in the office alone with a male, hiring a male is going to cause some difficulties for the workplace.*

As a pastor in an Evangelical church, I was often the only woman at pastors' meetings. I was at one meeting in which I needed to get a ride to the airport. There was this incredible awkward space of time when different men voiced their inability to help because they had a rule about being in a car alone with a woman. As this conversation unfolded, I felt a strange sense of shame arise within me. I had previously considered myself a colleague on equal footing. All of a sudden I was marked as something "other," and even more embarrassing, a sexual threat. A male colleague was able to step in and help out, which relieved the public tension, yet the private awareness of belonging had significantly shifted. Walls do separate.

These walls can also give an unfair advantage to men or women who report to a boss of the same gender. A friend of mine reviewed rules he had created to safeguard his marriage vows. He decided he would enforce those rules with all of his colleagues so that the women and men who worked for him had equal access. This is a tricky area, but we must be willing to review our personnel policies not only in light of our vulnerabilities but also in light of the implications those policies might have for all the people with whom we work. The influx of women in nontraditional roles demands that all of us have to face our issues regarding our sexuality and temptations in healthier ways. Sequestering men from women is not the way to resolve this issue. We must live out these concerns in such a way that space is provided for healthy and whole relationships with men and women.

The kingdom of God provides us an invitation to a reconciled relationship with God, with ourselves, with each other, and with our world. The beauty of this new relationship is expressed in Galatians 3: "As many of you as were baptized in Christ have clothed yourselves with Christ. There is no longer Jew or Greek, there is no longer slave or free, there is no longer male and female; for all of you are one in Christ Jesus" (Galatians 3:27-28).

I remember telling two male colleagues they were my "girlfriends." Their faces were all awry as they tried to figure out what I meant. I explained that the life we shared together was honest, true, and fun, and that outside of my relationship with my husband, I had primarily experienced that with girlfriends. They gingerly accepted this as a compliment. I appreciate the richness men and women bring into my life, and I would not want to lose out on receiving the gift of each person with whom I work and live. Ruth Barton says it so well:

> Mutually empowering relationships are those in which we enable or permit others to be powerful in our lives and in the lives of others in good, kingdom-building ways. In such relationships we invite strength and spiritual influence to flow unblocked from one to the other.[9]

A gift-based calling would give us all breathing space to be true to who we are and what God has placed on our hearts. Romans 12 seems fairly simple and yet glorious when in essence we are told:

> Let the singers sing,

Let the teachers teach,
Let the artist create,
Let the builders build,
And let the leaders lead.

Clearly this has potential for a much more chaotic identity process. If my gender does not determine my vocation, then all possibilities are open. This wide horizon also means I have to get to know myself and others in a more intimate way than a preconceived role definition would provide. This demands more internal and external work than previously demanded of us. There will be messy times as we work out our vocation and identity. Yet there is beauty in this deeper level of knowing. We can celebrate each other not by how we fulfill a role but by how we fulfill our call.

Maybe in the Christian community we could even begin to move from asking each other about our jobs as a way of getting to know one another to asking each other about how God is speaking and leading. I have a great friend who was a stay-at-home mom when her boys were growing up. Since they have grown, she has continued to follow God's call in caring for elderly persons in her church, caring for ill family members, offering herself as a caring presence to young girls who need a mother figure. She is always prayerfully listening to God. Yet she is often put in the position of feeling as if she has to defend her existence when she is asked what she does for a living. She said she often receives odd looks when she tries to describe how she spends her time.

Some men and women sense they are being devalued when they are working in areas not typically male or female or when they are without a specific job because their call escapes those confines or they are waiting for God to lead them in new directions. We need better questions to ask each other if the purpose is to find true intimacy.

This freedom to celebrate each other's gifts and callings helps move all of us into egalitarian relationships where we value each other. This then invites us into relationships of non-dominance instead of superiority, but there is an interdependency that collectively reflects God's image. A woman participating in leadership, therefore, frees not only women with those gifts to fulfill their life's calling—it also should free men to pursue their callings in all the wondrous forms that occur. A man in the daycare, a woman as the pastor, a man as an artist, a woman caring for children in her home are each a beautiful manifestation of God's call if it is fulfilled according to the gifts and graces given to them. We also have to allow for fluidity in the pursuit of responding to God's call.

This freedom allows people to move into new roles of leadership that open up in unexpected ways. Women by choice or socialization often don't aspire to leadership roles but find themselves growing into those roles as they step into areas of service in civic or church settings. Most men receive their education, enter into the workforce in their particular field, and move through the ranks at varying degrees. Some men need permission to explore different paths along the way. Women have most often taken a circuitous path. They volunteer at a local level. Then, as they take on greater responsibilities, they begin to interface with those who have more official power in that line of work. This interface often opens their eyes to envision themselves in leadership in that area, or, in some cases, frustration with the leadership causes them to begin to consider entering the decision-making arena as they grow deeper in their knowledge of themselves, God, and their world. Freedom to discover and grow allows men and women to make life changes that encourage them to flourish.

There can be seasons of life in which the vocational fulfillment of God's work shifts and changes. We must allow space for growth, change, and personal discoveries that direct and redirect each other's paths. It is this space that sets men and women free to respond to God's call in life-giving ways. This is life-giving for the individual and for the community as a whole.

FOUR

# GOD'S SONG OF PRAISE

*The Lord your God is with you, he is mighty to save.*
*He will take great delight in you, he will quiet you with his love,*
*he will rejoice over you with singing.*
—Zephaniah 3:17, NIV

❧❧❧

❧ As persons who are responding to God's call to leadership, we often miss out on the celebration that occurs over our lives. Zephaniah 3:17 reminds us of God's singing over us, God's delight over us, and God's celebration over us. I don't think this image has truly sunk into the deepest places of my being. When I read the story of the prodigal son found in the Gospel of Luke, I understand the celebration feast over the return of one who was lost and considered dead. I have joyfully joined church celebrations of those who have shared testimonies of repentance and returning to God. There were even times as a young person when I was jealous of the dramatic conversion stories some people had experienced, obviously not comprehending the depth of the pain and chaos inherent in those stories.

I am perhaps more like the elder son than I would like to admit. Hopefully I am not as judgmental toward my brothers and sisters as he seemed to be. But I do stumble over the father's response to the elder: "Son, you are always with me, and all that is mine is yours" (Luke 15:31). There is something within me that still needs to compare. Is this joy of shared life as big and broad and meaningful as the banquet for the prodigal? Something in here reminds me of my childhood desire for fairness. If someone gets praise for getting a B on an exam, then certainly there should be louder praise for getting an A! This, of course, misses the opportunity to understand the particular challenges in obtaining either grade—by child or content—or the beauty inherent in what one may have learned in the process.

For the purposes of our reflection, the older son represents Christians in leadership. I am not so concerned about the jealousy and anger he expresses toward his prodigal brother. Instead, I would like to ponder the anger rooted in a lack of understanding of the love and celebration the father has always held in his heart for him.

The elder son has offered his body, mind, and soul in service to his father. Somehow the elder son missed the joy this brought his father. Somehow the elder son did not understand the love that had been poured out over him as he lived his life in obedience. Somehow he missed the singing and delight and celebration. We might think the father's understated joy over the older son is in stark contrast to the party for the prodigal. That surely helps create this crisis moment.

Yet I suggest we miss the depth of the father's delight in the older son. We miss the richness found in their shared life with all its laughter, tears, and true substance. "Shared life" is a domestic term that is largely made up of the mundane—the meals to be cooked and cleared, the bills to be paid, the chores to be done. It also includes the celebratory events that are sprinkled across days of mundane. The fullness of the intimacy is found in small events—shared meals, laughing over life's absurdities, the common work of creating a home. It is the daily bread of life. Leadership is filled with such work, and we can miss God's delight as we work out conflicts in the workplace, create systems that function more efficiently, inspire others to fulfill their vocations, and even when we absorb the criticisms that come with leadership. We can lose our sense of joy in the mundane, for the beauty of our service to God is seen only with a much larger view of the whole.

In addition to potentially losing our joy in the mundane, we can as leaders sometimes think of our movement into positions of authority as self-serving. Again, we do not experience our God's joy that we are living out the leadership gifts given us. Instead, we can think of our growing confidence as perhaps a bit prideful. Others may offer similar critiques. These critics can assume any movements into leadership can mean only a self-serving upward mobility. We split off acts of service to God into narrowly defined acts of piety. While we need to practice the spiritual disciplines, which include prayer, meditation, and caring for oppressed populations, God's joy is found also in exercising our gifts to lead.

This separation from God's joy in our leadership can leave some leaders with a dichotomous experience. It not only means they experience God's joy in only a small percentage of their lives—it also means that they can sometimes fail to seek the wisdom of God in their acts as leaders. This can lead some seemingly "good church folk" to make God-denying decisions in their workplace.

We can miss out on God's joy because we cannot accept our abilities or worthiness to lead. We can suffer because we live in fear that others will discover that we are imposters as leaders. We are victims of false comparisons to the seemingly perfect leadership of others. We are all too aware of our own foibles and weaknesses. We can be consumed with protecting our identity as successful leaders, unable to admit mistakes for fear that the tenuous foundation will fall apart. We can alternatively undermine our own leadership potential by not accepting new leadership roles because we have unrealistic concerns about our leadership skills. Nouwen described one young man who struggled as an elder son:

> For years he had walked around with the inner questions: "Does anyone really love me? Does anyone really care?" And every time he had climbed a little higher on the ladder of success, he had thought: "This is not who I really

am; one day everything will come crashing down and then people will see that I am no good."[1]

Joy can be found when we offer ourselves to the opportunities of leadership with an abandon of service to God and others. This kind of abandon demands a certain looseness in the way we hold on to any position. The position must never define you. Your life is instead defined by being centered in the love of God for you and for others. Any position is simply a platform for your service to God. The position can change while the heart intent remains the same. Vocational decisions certainly include discernment, using prayer, personal assessment, and good counsel from trusted friends.

Leadership positions are not embraced as earned rewards but opportunities to serve. In this attitude we can revel in the gifting God has poured in and through our lives, and we move from fear to celebration. If we understand our entrance into leadership as expressions of our worship of God, we might hear the song of joy when we serve in this way. If we see our obedient walk in following God's call into places of leadership as beautiful as the repentant walk of the returning prodigal, we might know God's joy over our lives. And if we offer our lives as a song of praise, an expression of our love, we might be more tuned in to hear God's song surrounding us. In this way we change the story of the elder son from one of anger and frustration to one who is ready to celebrate every story of redemption.

The larger context of God's joy expressed in Zephaniah comes with words of warning. The whole of Zephaniah 3, and even the two chapters preceding it, repeatedly use two words: *woe* and *judgment*.

What do we do with these words? Is there good news to be found? We can be comfortable with the *woe* language as long as it is turned to someone else. In Zephaniah one people group or country after another hears this message of judgment. Yet it is fairly common in Scripture that when the religious folk get comfortable with admonitions toward others, the woe turns in on them. Adding to the shock that occurs when the woe turns in on the listener is that the surprise critique is usually at a heightened level of harshness. We are, after all, a people who have heard from God, received the words of God, made commitments to God, been set apart by God, and made claims still to be serving God. And yet a woe is proclaimed to the city of oppressors, rebellious and defiled, to the people of Jerusalem. And many in Jerusalem would be surprised to be called such things. "Certainly the Philistines are these things, as well as those Assyrians, but not us," would probably be the response.

If denial stops and honest reflection begins, we can discover the steps to being oppressors, rebellious and defiled, found in this passage. These steps are found in Zephaniah 3:2: "It has listened to no voice; it has accepted no correction. It has not trusted in the LORD; it has not drawn near to its God."

This causes me to pause. This rebellion didn't come about by a choice to leave like the prodigal son or by a decision not to live for God. It is simply done by the hardening of the heart one step at a time; a journey the elder son might have replicated. The woe and judgment is that Jerusalem is not fulfilling the purpose for which she was created—steps I recognize in my own spirit. She has listened to no voice. She accepts no correction. She does not trust in the Lord. She does not draw near to God.

The disappointment is not just because this rebellion has occurred but also because God created Jerusalem for more than this. Jerusalem was to be a city that shined as a witness to God. Jerusalem has gifts and graces that were to be a proclamation of the presence of God. Jerusalem needed to live out her full calling. I think God is saying that to a lot of us. God says it when we get too busy to draw near, when we make decisions and then ask for God's blessings as an afterthought. God says it when we are consumed with personal success and when we walk blindly past the sick, the poor, and the hungry. He says it when we take our gifts and graces for leadership and refuse to use them for

His glory. God is relentless, for He calls us by name and continues to say, *I have made you for more than this.*

Attending women's clergy conferences across the years has exposed me to a plethora of stories that reflect this reality. Many women talked about their early sense that God was calling them to pastoral leadership. This calling was either never named or quickly squelched by their faith communities. The calling went underground. These women sought other avenues of service. A college student recently shared the ongoing nature of this story. She told her pastor when she was little that she was called to be a pastor. The pastor's response was to inform her she was not hearing right since that was not a woman's call. She repeated this call a few years later and was told again that this could not be true. Again she repeated the call in her teen years with her youth group. This time she was told that clearly her call was to be the wife of a youth pastor. It was in college that she heard a professor say that women are called as preachers as well. She was then set free to reclaim this early sense of vocation.

For the older women I encountered at these conferences, it was a much longer journey of pushing the call down but having it bubble up at intermittent times throughout their lives. As one friend described it, "It was an itch that could not be scratched away." For these women, entering into ministry was a joyous release as they moved past this barrier that had existed between them and experiencing the fullness of God's work in them.

What is it that gets in the way of fulfilling what we are created by God to know and live? Ultimately, whatever hinders us from living out the life of God among the people of God is sin. This can be personal sin, corporate sin, or systemic sin. When we speak of the inhibiting power of personal sin, we often talk about morality issues. Some will talk about issues of obedience regarding life vocation. It is important for our definition of sin to include any commitment, behavior, or obstacle that would hinder our living out the full life of God. There can be a plethora of hinderances: rebellion, issues of self-esteem, personal or community squelching of God's work in and through our lives. Phoebe Palmer's call to put "all on the altar" included the relinquishment of dependency on others, a limitation of an expression of our gifts, and relational idolatry.[2]

This radical obedience creates a freedom from internal and external inhibitors that would limit the fullest expression of God's gifts and graces evidenced in our lives. This in no way means that we are to trash relationships or deny the significant counsel of others. It is to challenge each of us to know that our first devotion is to God. This can be fully expressed only when we are freed to respond to God's call with an honest naming of our giftedness, which includes leadership and preaching.[3]

Women who enter into pastoral ministry find a necessary detachment from the obstacles, both interior and exterior, to their sense of call. This detachment is coupled with a growing attachment to hear what God has been stirring deep in their souls. Many women talk about a moment in a worship service, leadership conference, or confession to a senior pastor or friend that loosed them to name this unchanging call. Something within their souls was set free. These words from a song entitled "Noble Purpose" echo this commitment:

> I want to live a life, Lord, that's worthy of my call.
> I want to live a life, Lord, that's worthy of my call
> And I believe you can change me.
> And I believe you can use this life.
> And I believe you can make me
> An instrument for noble purpose.
>
> Take my life, I give it all to You my King
> Be Glorified in me, in each joy, each suffering
> Here I am, Here I am, this is my everything.
> My life will be a song of praise.

And may that song be heard for all my days: "Use me, Lord. Use me."[4]

53

The road to this level of church leadership continues to have challenges for these women. And yet the assurance and naming of their call created new space to know God's joy. This newfound joy calls us to remember the verse in Zephaniah: "Sing aloud, O daughter Zion; shout, O Israel! Rejoice and exult with all your heart, O daughter Jerusalem!" (Zephaniah 3:14).

There is incredible joy when we are free to know the fullness of God's call realized in our life's work. God has made each of us to be a people of song—certainly in lifting our voices in praise, but more importantly, we are called to live *lives* that sing out with kindness, justice, and faithfulness, sing out with peace, generosity, and hope, sing out with the freedom for our particular voice to join the resounding praise of angels and archangels.

Paul's letter to the Romans describes this life song as the body living in praise to God as the prophets prophesy, the teachers teach, the givers give, the leaders lead. It is like a choir tuning its voices and then moving into one beautiful, harmonious sound. Zephaniah indicates that as we sing out, living the life of our calling, if we pause we might hear the responding song of God over us. To know the fullness of this song our hearts must be in tune to God's calling, and God's unique creation of our particular voice.

Mosquitoes actually provide us an illustration. Studies have been done on their mating patterns. The male and female match up only when the musical notes made by their wings create a perfect chord. The male adjusts his tone to match the song of his mate.[5]

The fulfillment of this relationship is found only when their individual songs can make music together. As we tune our lives to the song of God, not only is our song made more beautiful but we also enter into this grand chorus with God that joins the song of the heavens. It is quite beautiful to imagine the gathering of modulations as God calls out these songs from each of us. A full song demands the breath, strength, and freedom to offer all of who we are in a responsive song of thanks to God. We receive the whispers of God's songs of mercy, we respond with a growing song of thanks, and God's song joins and surrounds us in celebration.

When we accept no correction, do not trust in God, and do not draw near or do not live the lives we were created to live, we simply fall out of tune, not out of grace. I think God's grace embraces those times of confusion, but we do fall into the space and place where God says, "I have made you for more than this." We are made for this great responsive song with our God. The call is again to "Sing aloud, O daughter Zion. Shout, O Israel. Rejoice and exult with all your heart, O daughter Jerusalem!" (Zephaniah 3:14). And the promise is "The LORD your God is with you, he is mighty to save. He will take great delight in you, he will quiet you with his love, he will rejoice over you with singing" (Zephaniah 3:17, NIV).

This passage reveals different types of songs God offers over us as we lead. Each song is an expression of love. The different types of songs do reflect God's responsiveness to the everydayness of our leadership tasks. There are times and seasons when God offers songs of delight and rejoicing and songs of quiet or lullabies.

We can hear songs of rejoicing when dreams are fulfilled and glimpses of the fullness of God are known. One church I served as pastor had a great potential that was coupled with low expectations and fear by the general church membership. As I believed and painted for the church what I saw as a strong mission and future, there were many who doubted. There was no huge life-changing event, and growth sometimes felt painstakingly slow, both in deep discipleship and in numerical growth. I often referred to it as the two-step-forward-one-step-back dance. I am not a particularly splashy pastoral leader. One Sunday—not an Easter or Christmas—the sanctuary was packed with people, the music was spilling out before the service began, and there was messy, chaotic life all around. A layperson in the church stood next to me and looked about in wonderment and said, "So this is what you have been talking about." The song of praise I heard in that moment was of great rejoicing—not for what any one person had done but for the vision of God being realized. It was the vision of the prodigal, the elder son, and the father singing a song of joy over each other. I would call this God's song of rejoicing. It is in God, through God, and in response to God this cacophonous song is sung.

Another member of that church shared with me her experience one Sunday. She was sitting in the back of the sanctuary enjoying the gathering of the people as the service began. She said she felt powerful, holy love fill her in a new way. She looked about and was filled with love for each person there, those whose stories she knew well and those who she had yet to know. This holy love was for her God and for herself as she was part of this local expression of the church. A song was bursting in her soul with thankfulness for God leading her to this place and for what God was doing in this place. This fullness was an expression of God's holy love filling her anew. And this is a song of God's delight.

The last kind of song is a quieter expression of God's singing over us. For as we share the daily life of serving God and being a community formed by God, we experience times of disturbance and pain. I am thankful for the times I heard a song of lullaby being sung over me in the midst of loss and despair. This was a song of rest and assurance. This is a song that reminds me again that when the church is filled and when the church is empty, God delights over me. This song quiets me.

Even in the painful times, God's delight is over us as we seek to live in obedience to the tasks and the gifts that are part of that day. It is often the lullaby that calls me to the holy detachment from even my best visions to receive the amazingly grace-filled love of God that is for me and for all His people. There is great tenderness in God's song over us that ultimately reminds us that His delight is over us, not what we achieve.

Like a parent, He rejoices over every good gift we get to experience. He delights over our love for Him, each other, and for ourselves. And He pulls us into a full embrace and quiet song of love when we are in need.

God's intimate knowledge of every leader's potential is similar to His knowledge of Jerusalem. We are created to fulfill that which we are gifted to be. He calls us from those distractions. He sings a song of grace and mercy. He sings a song of love over His creation. And when we sing like the daughters of Zion, when we fearlessly shout aloud, filled with gladness and rejoicing, the promise is "The Lord your God is with you, he is mighty to save. He will take great delight in you, he will quiet you with his love, he will rejoice over you with singing" (Zephaniah 3:17, NIV).

# FIVE

# THE HEALING OF THE LEADER

*Are any among you suffering? They should pray. Are any cheerful?*
*They should sing songs of praise. Are any among you sick? They should call*
*for the elders of the church and have them pray over them,*
*anointing them with oil in the name of the Lord.*

—James 5:13-14

❧❧❧

❧ My journey with anointing with oil for healing began at the request of a member at the first church I pastored. A woman who suffered with painful arthritis called and asked if I could come and anoint her with oil. I said that I would love to, of course, and when I hung up the phone I started frantically looking for some resource for this practice. This had not been part of my church tradition nor had it been a practice discussed in my ministry classes in seminary. It was before the time of Internet search engines, so I gave a quick call to my father, who was also a pastor. He directed me to James 5:13-16:

Are any among you suffering? They should pray. Are any cheerful? They should sing songs of praise. Are any among you sick? They should call for the elders of the church and have them pray over them, anointing them with oil in the name of the Lord. The prayer of faith will save the sick, and the Lord will raise them up; and anyone who has committed sins will be forgiven. Therefore confess your sins to one another, and pray for one another, so that you may be healed.

The simple liturgy my father provided that day was to read the scripture, explain that the invitation to this prayer is for God's healing as God chooses and to offer anointing with these words: "In accordance with scripture in the name of the Father, Son, and Holy Spirit I anoint [insert name] with oil for healing." This phrase could then be followed with more specificity regarding the person's need.

As I came into the woman's house with my vial of oil, I prayed for God's leading and blessing. It was a little awkward, as any first-time experiences can be. I read the passage, she knelt at her worn, flowered chair, and I followed the liturgy as my father had explained. I anointed her forehead with oil (probably a little more oil than necessary), and prayed.

It was simple and amazingly beautiful. From that first experience through every time I have anointed or received anointing, I have sensed the powerful healing presence of God. This has not often manifested itself in a physical healing. Far more profound is the holy sense of God's healing presence that soothes the soul.

My engagement with the practice of anointing with oil for prayer has only increased over time. The years in the pastorate have deepened my knowledge of the need for healing in everyone's life from past, present, and future concerns. At one church where I served, several identified themselves as "wounded healers." They were profoundly impacted by Henri Nouwen's book of that same title. There was much brokenness among the members of the congregation due to both family and church family dysfunctions. Nouwen's description in the 1970s of a generation characterized by "inwardness, fatherlessness and convulsiveness"[1] rang true for this particular group. Some of the members may have connected to the wounded identity to their detriment. There were times when I felt we shared more pain than healing, more woundedness than hope. This was something that in time began to change, but not without plenty of hard conversations, prayer, and time for growth.

The reality of these wounds has only become truer. As I work with college students in my present ministry, I still see them profoundly working through these same characteristics—perhaps because they are the age now to be the original congregation's children. Inwardness, fatherlessness, and convulsiveness continue to be known in this new generation. As people, they are clearly much more than these characteristics; they are also optimistic, engaged, loving, and responsive. Yet pain caused by the first three characteristics is evident, and the need for healing is shared by all.

Across the years in many different locations I have engaged in the practice of anointing with oil for healing, staying basically to the same format. The anointing oil is sometimes offered through my prayers and sometimes offered by another leader in the church. This creates space in which I both give and receive these prayers. It is an intentional act to model the need for all God's people to receive God's healing work in our lives. As a pastor-leader I have found these prayers often free me to forgive, to heal, to have courage, to repent, to stay spiritually healthy in the strife of loving and leading a church. This healing prayer is a waterfall of grace over my soul.

Leadership can be a lonely place. Leadership demands that you make decisions for the whole of the organization that at times are not pleasing to individuals. This creates distance between you and the people who work under your leadership. In addition, leadership puts you in a place of receiving confidential information. There are reasons behind decisions made or directions charted that you cannot fully divulge to all interested parties. If you are going to keep confidences, you will absorb a lot of pain. I heard one denominational leader talk about his recovery after leadership. Once he stepped down from the leadership position, he realized just how many wounds he still had from working with churches in crisis. He had not realized how many arrows had gone deep into his being. He finally had space in his schedule to be quiet and to realize how many wounds were still bleeding and needed healing.

I had one staff person who confronted a member once and began appropriately naming some issues but then said, "I am going to take my pastor hat off now and just talk to you from my experience." Obviously he and I had a conversation about the impossibility of that move. You can never completely take off your identity as pastor/leader with members of your church or organization. You can be real, vulnerable, and share life in deep ways. Yet there are still things, especially in the toughest of times, you cannot talk about. Speaking openly about some conflicts in an organization would only make the situation more volatile. Confidentiality and appropriateness often prevent the leader from fully defending herself or himself. When you are in conflict with lay leadership, it is inappropriate to bring that to the general church body. It is necessary and vital to have an outside confidant to process the pastoral/leadership experience.

Leading into times of change inevitably means taking all the leadership hits that come with that journey. Every pastor-leader has been misunderstood, misaligned, or misrepresented. There is general pain in the life of the pastor/leader, and it is the ongoing work of that person to forgive and continue to lead. In a study of churches led through times of change, the leader inevitably encountered conflict and pain.[2]

It is important for leaders to walk into painful situations with their eyes open and their hearts prepared. The alternative is to settle for something far less than fulfilling the God-given potential for your particular church or organization. Rainer gave a significant challenge for leaders tempted to pull back because of pain. "We must lead. Yes, we must love the people, and we must console them when change becomes increasingly painful to them. But we must lead. We cannot be content with a life and a ministry that could be described in the epitaph: 'This leader avoided conflict well.'"[3]

I recently served on a panel of pastors who were asked to respond to the question "What do you wish they had told you in seminary?" Each person came up with unique perspectives, but shared across the panel was the painful journey with some church people as they sought to lead. My synopsis was "Good leadership equals hate mail." Some laypeople will question every change. Others who support you initially may withdraw their support when you are unable to give your approval to their plan or program. Many just don't know how to stay and work through relationships when there are disagreements. The leader is often confronted with weighing a decision, knowing that whichever direction he or she goes, there will be fallout. The leader often needs good counsel to help stay focused on what is best for all rather than what is preferred by a few.

As leaders, we will be the lightning rod for pain during times of change. As mentioned earlier, praying The Lord's Prayer has been a life-giving practice in my leadership. The great church prayer, "Lord have mercy" is also life-giving as I recognize the need for mercy in all our lives. Forgiveness is daily; it is common; it is necessary. It is not easy. I have found the only way to forgive is to receive the healing flow of grace over my life again and again. The reality that difficult people will continue to be in the leader's life in ways that are disruptive means that the work is ongoing. Forgiveness is a complicated, messy call for any Christian. In a later chapter we will walk through this call as a leader in more detail. It is important now to affirm that personal healing is a vital part of living out forgiveness. Consistent prayer for healing helps us do this daily, common, and necessary work.

Add to this layer of general life pain the particular experiences of a *woman* in leadership, and the work of healing and forgiveness calls us to even deeper places. To be a woman in leadership in the Evangelical tradition means there is some level of pain you experience simply because of your gender. Some women have experienced this nominally; some have experienced it in soul-crushing ways. All have a need for healing. Stories abound of people who refuse to receive communion from a woman's hands, questions asked during the ordination process never asked of a man, isolation at meetings, jokes at their spouse's expense, opportunities given to those less qualified, dismissive comments about ideas and capabilities. These experiences can be overt where women are told they do not belong in leadership. Some women experience the unsettling realization that their ideas and contributions are not valued.

One friend who served on a staff as a ministry leader told about her experience of offering ideas or program revisions to the leadership team. She said it took her a while to realize that what she offered was almost immediately dismissed, but when a male colleague picked up the idea later in the meeting, it was affirmed. She eventually stepped down from this leadership position as she found it such a hard place to work and maintain good relationships.

The old spiritual "There Is a Balm in Gilead" speaks about this need for healing. The language is archaic, yet its meaning is profound. One time I heard it sung in a worship service with a question mark. "Is there a balm in Gilead?" It was a haunting question that echoed dramatically across the stone-walled chapel. It clearly reverberated even more dramatically in the hearts of the congregation as we considered different scenarios in which healing was needed. I sat as a first year seminarian student and received the question over my context then as I struggled with issues of faith and doctrine. The question is asked by many a leader tied to a specific time and place in which conflict and pain have arisen. To live and love is to experience hurt. All who have been hurt in the midst of leadership have asked themselves in some way the haunting question, *Is there a balm in Gilead?*

We sang this spiritual in one church, and afterward one of our visitors asked us why we were singing about "bombs." This word confusion can reveal an alternative response to healing balms in times of pain. The temptation is to verbally *bomb* a community in times of controversy, challenge, hurt, and pain. Once again the leader is challenged not to react to all the verbal mudslinging that occurs but to remain a non-anxious presence that steers the conversation and group to fulfill its mission and call. In the midst of leading, verbal explosions hurt and wound the leader's body, mind, and spirit. Healing is needed on all those levels.

The other temptation is to remove ourselves from the pain, guard our hearts, and let cynicism reign. I have talked with leaders who have fallen to both temptations. Hansen, in his book *The Art of Pastoring,* describes the gut-wrenching pain that occurs when people you have loved, believed in, and poured yourself into turn against you. This pain has left me curled up on the floor praying in ways that only the Holy Spirit can interpret. No matter how many ways you review what you could have done differently or how the process could have been healthier, ultimately with some people this explosion is an unstoppable train.

These train wrecks occur in every leader's life, because a leader represents authority. Authority figures receive the transference of all sorts of unresolved issues in people's lives. Hansen calls this "transference hell" and says we have three options:

1. Leave the ministry,

2. Stay in the ministry but stop loving people (and become a religious hack), or

3. Grow up.[4]

Many people have chosen to leave the ministry or quit leadership. Growing up is hard. It involves loving those who express hatred toward you. It means treating fairly people who treat you unfairly, speaking in ways that set boundaries while valuing the person as a son or daughter of God. It means moving beyond the personal to a much larger view of the person and the issue.

No one does this perfectly. Every leader can grow through the most challenging of times. The only way I know to grow up is to lean on God for the healing that is needed in my spirit, that I might love the most destructive of persons in my life. This love does include setting healthy boundaries as we live in community. Nevertheless, Christian leadership remains engaged in relationships. To continue in relational commitment means that you as a leader are marked with vulnerability. Nouwen talks about this as an appropriate martyrdom:

The beginning and end of all Christian leadership is to give your life for others. Thinking about martyrdom can be an escape unless we realize that real martyrdom means a witness that starts with the willingness to cry with those who cry, laugh with those who laugh, and to make one's own painful and joyful experiences available as sources of clarification and understanding."[5]

This journey demands vulnerability that makes some level of pain inevitable and healing an ongoing necessity.

So what does it mean to receive this balm of Gilead? Balm is a healing ointment that takes away the sting and protects against infection. Gilead was a region in the Transjordan. The writer of the spiritual took this question from Jeremiah 8:22—"Is there no balm in Gilead? Is there no physician there? Why then has the health of my poor people not been restored?" The context of this passage leads into a lament over the destruction of Jerusalem. Jeremiah 46:11 says, "Go up to Gilead, and take balm, O virgin daughter Egypt! In vain you have used many medicines; there is no healing for you."

You can hear in that context that the implied answer is, no, there is no balm at that time of lament. There is no healing in this time and space. This, however, is not the last word. The author of this spiritual has a broader view and points the hearer to the ultimate answer regarding a balm to be found in Jesus Christ.

This emphatic no and yes ring true in my own life. There are places where healing waters seem to flow. I can enter into the homes of certain friends and know this is going to be a place where I am loved, prayed over, and given the food of life, both literally and metaphorically. But there are also places where no healing is to be found. Some event or poison has so marked a place or community that healing is not within its waters. Ultimately the healing is found by the outpouring of God's spirit upon the person or persons involved. In both kinds of places healing is found in the presence of God at work. Sometimes God uses important others to help move us forward from these times of pain and distress. Other times this healing is received by the Holy Spirit's ministry over a chaotic soul.

The promise that runs from the Creation story throughout Scripture is that God can take the most chaotic scene, the driest bones, and the utterly lost and do a new thing. The importance of reaching out for this healing touch is vital in helping us to lead from a place of assurance, hope, and grace. The healing of God's presence protects us from reactive temptations such as anger, isolation, abandonment, and blame.

As I recently read again the lyrics of this spiritual, I was surprised at how much the pain is connected to leadership questions and insecurities. As a leader, take a moment to read these great words:

> *Sometimes I feel discouraged,*
> *And think my work's in vain,*
> *But then the Holy Spirit*
> *Revives my soul again.*
>
> *There is a balm in Gilead*
> *To make the wounded whole;*
> *There is a balm in Gilead*
> *To heal the sin-sick soul.*
>
> *If you cannot preach like Peter,*
> *If you can't pray like Paul,*
> *You can tell the love of Jesus*
> *And say, "He died for all."*[6]

Every leader at some point is both discouraged and convinced that his or her work is in vain. Often, even with great encouragers in our lives, the reviving presence of God is the only healer. This healing is like a gift of oxygen for starved lungs. In times of leadership distress we can feel as if the breaths we take are only shallow attempts. In the presence of God, the wonder and life-giving attributes of deep, lung-filling breaths can return. Depending upon the severity of the situation, this renewed ability to breathe can come in several ways.

An important source of healing for a leader is to take Sabbath rests. We all struggle to find ways to create these spaces. Days of rest help us move from the particulars of our work to see the larger scene. I have the privilege of being able to see the Pacific Ocean through my office window. I have to remind myself to take little Sabbaths in the midst of the day and look out across the horizon. Somehow that puts the irritations of leadership in a much better perspective. Creating rhythms of days of rest and spiritual retreats is significant for someone who wants to maintain healthy leadership for the long haul. Sabbaths remind us that we are not God; the work of this world does not depend upon us.

Taking a Sabbath also helps us honor those who work for us. We relinquish areas of our work to the capable leadership of others. In more severe times of burnout, Sabbaths may come with more intentional focus on healing and renewal. Retreats, sabbaticals, and space for enrichment through classes and conferences can all be helpful tools for healing in the midst of leadership.

The second stanza speaks to the personal limitations that we all feel. Certainly no Christian can claim to preach like Peter and pray like Paul, as well as dance like Miriam (especially those of us from a Holiness church tradition). We can spend a lot of time beating ourselves up for our lack of perfection at every task. The greatest promise we have as Christians is that we can lift to God those concerns regarding our limitations and know that He fills and uses us beyond our capabilities.

We, of course, can be our own harshest critics. Sometimes the healing we need is from our self-criticizing ways. We hurt our work when we spend time comparing ourselves *to* rather than learning *from* those who are good models of leadership. We may not be able to run a meeting or communicate a vision as others we have observed can, but we can grow in our abilities, we can become more confident in how we do it differently, and we might do other things better. Every leadership position will engage us in tasks at which we naturally excel; other tasks we will find more challenging. Peace is found when we become comfortable with our limitations and simply live out Christ's redemptive call on our lives. This doesn't excuse us from always being engaged and learning as we do the work we are called to do, but we don't have to be defensive about not being great at everything. It is vital for Christian leaders to become comfortable with the gifts and graces they have for their work as well as knowledgeable about areas in which they might need the help of others.

It is a healing process to grow comfortable in your own skin. Nouwen puts it this way: "As soon as we feel at home in our own house, discover the dark concerns as well as the light spots, the closed doors as well as the drafty rooms, our confusion will evaporate, our anxiety will diminish, and we will become capable of creative work."[7] Deep breaths can return as we receive healing over false expectations.

It is important that leaders also recognize what brings healing to the soul. A friend of mine who served as an advocate for children with a state government made sure she spent one morning a week volunteering at a children's center. This time with children gave her new breath as she dealt with state legislation and bureaucracies. In pastoral leadership it was vital for me to step out of the church and serve in one of our compassionate ministry centers or share life and the good news of

Christ with a neighbor. Engaging in this way gave me new energy and purpose as I returned to the work of administration and church life. Outside interests—a walk on the beach, a hike in the mountains, a quiet space to read—can bring healing. It is important to find renewing, breath-of-God moments in our schedules.

It is also important to have some level of self-understanding to discover what renews you and what drains you. An introvert engaged in a people-intense work environment must find solitude to regroup. An extravert in a task-intensive work environment has to create places of interaction with others to renew. We must each create life rhythms that offer renewal and healing in order to be fulfilled in a leadership role.

# SIX

# RECEIVING POWER

*Fear not, for I have redeemed you; I have called you by name; you are mine. When you pass through waters, I will be with you; and when you pass through the rivers, they will not sweep over you. When you walk through fire, you will not be burned; the flames will not set you ablaze.*

—Isaiah 43:1-2, NIV

❦❦❦

❧ In recent years I have lived near Mexico, and I enjoy spending time south of the border with friends. A challenge to deepening some of these friendships is my total lack of ability to speak Spanish. When asked why I didn't learn this language, I found myself telling the sad tale of a horrible Spanish teacher from high school. At some point I realized how ridiculous this excuse is. Not only was my encounter with this teacher more than thirty years ago, but I also had another opportunity to learn Spanish in college, and I didn't take advantage of that opportunity either. I think it may be time to decide if I actually want to learn to speak Spanish and, if so, to begin to create and commit to the opportunities still available to me. It's time to stop blaming a past teacher and get on with my life.

There are moments when we recognize obstacles to our leadership and are able to identify systems that serve as blockades. These realities are true and must be addressed; yet we cannot allow them to define our lives, calling, and vocation. We must recognize the power that is ours through Christ and live our lives in ways not labeled by those obstacles.

Men and women who are called to leadership will encounter resistance. They may find themselves facing failure or dead ends. Leadership "opportunities" are sometimes veiled collision courses, and even the most gifted of us will not be able to salvage every situation. Given the issues of sexism that still pervade our culture, facing obstacles will be a relatively common experience for women. While those moments are often filled with disappointment, grief, and despair, there are also powerful choices to be made in response. We can remain trapped and become increasingly angry, or we can ask ourselves, *If not this, then what?* and begin to explore the various options that will become apparent.

I do not in any way want to diminish the pain that comes with this process. It is often unfair, unjust, and not at all how things should be. But remember: our lives are not surrendered to a particular church, system, or program. We are surrendered to God. It is important to give ourselves whatever space is needed to grieve, to knock, to confront, and even demand. Eventually we will need to enter a space with God where we ask Him, *If not this, then what?* and allow new discernment to direct our paths. It is the power of remembering that our Redeemer—our Savior—is Jesus Christ, not any person or system.

The opening words of Isaiah 43 help us hear this call to live boldly. The power to live such a life is to first be one who lives in assurance of God's redemption, calling, and steadfast presence in our lives. There will be days we are shut down, days we are silenced, days we are weary. Yet in the midst of these days we hear the repeated words of the messengers of God: "Fear not" (Isaiah 43:1, NIV). Over and over God's people are told to fear not as they offer what little they have to God and see what He can do with the simplest gifts. This is the message for the people of Israel, this is the message to Abraham, Joshua, and Gideon, and this is the message Mary received from the angel: "Fear not, for God is with you."

Part of receiving power from God is to be held responsible for how that power is used in our lives. I have heard myself and others claim powerlessness in certain situations. And yet upon reflection it is clear that while there may not have been power to change the situation completely, there was power to do something.

I love the title of a book that is the study of six New Testament women: *Do What You Have the Power to Do.*[1] That title takes away our excuses, and that can be scary. As we assess our present situations, we may have to make tough decisions, work toward new strategies and goals, forgive those in our past, and address personal patterns that hinder our personal and professional development. We can still address the limiting structures, but we must be creative and find ways around those structures. One colleague shared that she was never given the opportunity to pastor a church, so she started one. I don't get to blame a high school teacher for my lack of language skills. She's part of my story, but I make her a much larger force by letting her poor teaching many years ago rule my ability at this late date to speak Spanish.

In the Gospel of Mark we find the story of the woman who entered the house of Simon the leper and anointed Jesus (Mark 14:3-9). This is the story of a seemingly powerless, unnamed woman who entered uninvited and interrupted a meal to minister to Jesus. We cannot always wait for an invitation to fulfill our calling.

In our culture we can hear all sorts of derogatory names for women who seem pushy or aggressive. While our attitude must always be of Christ Jesus, we must be boldly confident even at the risk of being called those names. When this woman entered the room, she was treated rudely and criticized. Harsh words did not deter her commitment to action. In Mark's story she anointed the head of Jesus. She performed an act of hospitality usually provided by the host. She stood intimately close to Jesus and, in this case, rather than washing His feet, she anointed

His head with oil, symbolizing His role as Messiah. Her gracious act and personal assuredness caused an angry response in others but was affirmed by Jesus Christ. He told the others to leave her alone and said that she would be remembered for this act.

The good news is that Jesus is not interested in traditional gender roles, but He is deeply interested in faithful disciples—both male and female.

This woman had clearly been following Jesus. She had been watching Him and knew Him. Her actions in a place where women were to remain silent proclaimed loudly that she recognized something the disciples were still struggling to comprehend. She at least partially understood His anointing as Messiah as well as the imminent danger of His life.

Her response was extravagant. As she poured out the costly ointment, she also poured out her life in ministry to Christ. When she walked into that home, it was not about personal rights or self-serving elevation—it was to fulfill God's calling. She was obedient to the stirring of God that had called her to action. Pearson says it well; "Whatever prompted her action, the woman willingly went against the accepted place of women in her religion and culture, for she realized that the time to do something for Jesus was soon to be no more."[2]

She could have assumed powerlessness. She could have felt the internal witness that Jesus was the Messiah, and even the need to anoint, and still held back. She could have been at the door and realized this was a place she neither belonged nor was wanted and turned away. After His crucifixion and resurrection she could have told others, "I sensed I needed to anoint Jesus on that day, but I could not go in." And others would have nodded their heads in sad agreement. There are times when claims of powerlessness may be true, but they were not true for her on that day. Her story witnesses what Jesus affirms: "She has done what she could" (Mark 14:8).

Twelve-step programs and others have rightly named pow-erlessness as an important confession toward recovery from addiction. A more explicitly Christian context would be the im-portance of a confession of sin and our powerlessness to over-come sin on our own. We are powerless apart from Christ, but through Christ we receive the outpouring of forgiveness that allows us to live empowered lives no longer bound by sin.

It is important to share a word of caution and hope for those who claim powerlessness. There are certain addictions, sin, and situations over which we clearly are powerless without God's help. The caution is to not give up and stay bound by those pow-ers and principalities. The hope is the power of God available as we open our lives to the work of the Holy Spirit. This transform-ing work of God is evident as we ask for help, ask for forgiveness, and make the life-changing commitments to small changes. The "Serenity Prayer" often used by those in the twelve-step move-ment makes an important distinction between what we can change and what we cannot change. The prayer also puts this discernment in the context of a world that is marked by sin.

*God, give us grace to accept with serenity*
*the things that cannot be changed,*
*courage to change the things*
*which should be changed,*
*and the wisdom to distinguish*
*the one from the other.*
*Living one day at a time,*
*Enjoying one moment at a time,*
*Accepting hardship as a pathway to peace,*
*Taking, as Jesus did,*
*This sinful world as it is,*
*Not as I would have it,*
*Trusting that You will make all things right,*
*If I surrender to Your will,*
*So that I may be reasonably happy in this life,*
*And supremely happy with You forever in the next.*
*Amen.*[3]

A powerlessness that denies one the ability to make choices, create change, and challenge structures is a powerlessness that denies the freedom that is part of every person, even in the most oppressed communities. The choices may be unjustly limited, but there are choices. In the most extreme cases the choice may be only internal acceptance or rejection of external messages and limited outward responses. For those in relatively free societies, the claims to powerlessness are often overstated. Some who claim to have no power are attempting to claim no responsibility. This can be a person in leadership denying the informal power that can be used toward changes he or she cares to make. This can be the personal choice to stand up for a person or group that is being mistreated. This can be a dissenting word or a prophetic word when issues of justice are at risk. These moments certainly call upon discernment and may not be done perfectly. Yet we cannot hide behind presumed powerlessness when there is something we can do.

This call to recognize our power is important as we responsibly respond to the micro and macro context of our lives. As Pearson notes, "We cannot separate ourselves from the use of power either as individuals or a society or as a church. It is a fact of life. Power is the ability to achieve purpose—the capability for action."[4] To deny this power is to refuse to be agents of change in society, institutions, or family systems.

I encountered a woman who had repeatedly heard from her community and church that she was a powerless woman. It is a sad story of spiritualized messages that reinforced her own quiet nature that she wasn't supposed to speak up, and she especially wasn't supposed to confront men of authority. Even when those men allowed or perpetuated abuse on her daughters, she accepted their excuses, denials, and justifications. This is a complex story that involves much culpability.

Yet I will always remember the great grief she experienced as her daughters confronted not only the men who had caused great harm but also her for not doing anything to stop the horror. A story like this causes me to pray that God will help me see the systems in which I live. I must be willing to see with eyes wide open the potential implications of my assumed powerlessness.

⌐A traditional prayer of confession is one that acknowledges the need for forgiveness for what was said and left unsaid and what was done and left undone. Both active and passive culpability exist. When the woman just mentioned asked her daughter what she could have done, given all the things she couldn't change, her daughter simply said, "You could have taken my hand and walked out."⌐

The needed power is not just for those times of being shut down or shut out. The need for power is also when opportunities open and new tasks are given for us to tackle. In all levels of leadership we need a new sense of God's power to fill our inadequacies and fears.

The last church I had the privilege of pastoring had a regular Sunday morning prayer time. My husband and I were co-pastors and took turns preaching. One of our "prayer people" always prayed over the one who was to preach, that he or she would have "holy unction." I think this is a good prayer for every Christian. It is especially significant for the woman gifted in leadership who seeks to live out that call.

The word *unction* has roots in the language of anointing. The prayers were for a leader who was anointed by the Holy Spirit. They included an acknowledgement that whatever giftedness, prayer, and preparation a pastor might have brought to the preaching moment, and all of these are important, to truly bring the word of God to the people of God a fresh anointing of the Holy Spirit is required. When the church talks about a fresh anointing it is referring to a renewal of passion for the work God has given them to do and wisdom to do the work well.

We see a particularized nature of the need for this anointing in the preaching event. And yet as Christian leaders asked to speak in moments of vision-casting, staff-equipping, or crisis response, holy unction is desperately needed. All leaders know that ultimately they are reaching beyond their own personal wisdom, resources, and abilities. The challenge for some women is that they may assume that this not true for their male colleagues. As women we may believe the assertive and positive posture many male colleagues present is actually a true expression of what they feel. We are tempted to wait until we feel some elusive level of competency before taking on a new task or level of leadership. Yet if you really get to know most leaders (there are, of course, a few confident exceptions), they, too, move into leadership opportunities with a painful knowledge of their limitations and personal uncertainties.

The teaching of the Church is that the power of the Holy Spirit forms us in Christlikeness, breathes new life into our beings, and guides us as we seek to live the life of Christ. This power is not poured out on the believer for some limited goal of personal success. This power is for an ongoing incarnational awareness, that we may see God, know Him, and live for Him.

In a small group a member prayed that she would always have a sense of awe. This prayer stuck with me. Life and leadership is best lived out with a sense of awe, the glory of God which is in us, around us, behind us, and before us. This "holy unction" power is the very presence of God poured out on the believer that his or her gifts may be offered to the glory of God. There is no greater witness to the gospel than the person who is free to bring all of who he or she is (including leadership skills) into a fully bodied service and response to God.

In Susie Stanley's work, *Holy Boldness*, she explores the testimonies of early women preachers regarding God's power at work in their lives. She noted that these women "committed themselves to God through consecration and faith. In return, God empowered them to act in ways they never imagined."[5] This power freed them to preach, to give voice and action in response to issues of justice, to engage in activities that moved beyond gender roles. For these women it was not an issue of rights but of obedience—obedience in response to seeing God, knowing God, and living for God.

A walk with God should always lead us into places that catch us by surprise. This may mean that we find ourselves in situations we never imagined. Out of God's powerful love at work in my life, I have been stretched way out of what was comfortable. I have been broken in those places as I recognize personal ignorance, apathy, and a judgmental attitude working in my life. I have experienced God's strength at work in me as I have tackled tasks way beyond my capabilities. We will be called to stretch. To stretch is to grow, and to grow is to become more like Christ through and through. That often means breaking through traditional gender roles. Again, it is not ultimately about rights but about obedience. Where is God calling you?

Part of the celebration of God's call is that He knows the particular strengths, gifts, and potential of every person. My father-in-law, Cecil Paul, was a great man. At his funeral an amazing line of people came to greet the family. A repeated message from many was their thankfulness for his ability to help them dream dreams for their lives beyond their imaginations.

We come before God often with very narrow understanding of what can be done in and through our lives. God receives us, gives thanks for us, breaks us, and offers us to the world in great love. This fourfold movement engages us to consider anew what God might do in and through our lives.

The power of the Holy Spirit at work in our lives is not just for personal freedom and joy but also so that we might seek the personal freedom and joy of others. The leader's ability to be still before God allows him or her to prayerfully lead in ways that are generally focused on the greater good. This does not create perfect leadership. We all need space to make mistakes, grow, receive, and extend grace. Yet if someone were able to step back and look at the underlying themes of the Christian leader's work, it should be love for God and love for others. The work of the Holy Spirit is made evident by our love. More explicitly, "to love is to act intentionally, in response to God and others, to promote well-being. To say the same thing in other words, to love is to respond to the inspiration of others—especially God—and by that response effect genuine flourishing."[6] Therefore our lives must be committed to living in and through the love of God revealed in Jesus Christ that allows a growth in wholeness for self and for others.

The deep prayer of God's people is for "holy unction." The prayer arises from a hunger to know the power of God released in our world. We are hungry to see truly transformed lives. This prayer acknowledges that for one to be filled by God's Spirit, to be released into full obedience to God's call, is ultimately for the benefit of all.

People sometimes do not fully understand what the results of their prayers might be. As a teenager, I participated in a nondenominational youth group in which I heard the consistent message of God's call and the importance of our obedience. Yet when I named my call to preach and commitment to obey, the leader was a bit stunned. This calling did not fit into his paradigm of my role as a woman. Nevertheless, I believe God answered his deeper prayer that the students under his care would hear from God and obey. So it is with the prayers of the people. They call out for legitimate daughters of God who know and offer healing in His name, who walk into spaces uninvited, who ultimately live life boldly by the power and unction of the Holy Spirit.

Holy unction, boldness, faithfulness, and fearless persistence are all necessary characteristics for a woman to live out her call into places of leadership. There are always concerns about the toxic nature of power, and we will deal with those temptations in the next chapter. But for many women the first step is to own and recognize the power that is inherently theirs in Christ. If the ultimate call to all disciples is a surrendered life to God, then women must surrender their obedience to silencing structures and speak when God calls. Women must surrender a passive way of living and be held accountable for their response to God's voice. They must not squelch the power of God's Holy Spirit. They must let the Holy unction of God so fill them that out of service to God they enter rooms uninvited, act in ways untraditional, and speak the truth God has laid on their hearts. They will offend and cause some to grumble.

Yet these women will hear the affirmation of Jesus, who says, "She has done what she could" or, as the *Jerusalem Bible* reads, "She has done what was in her power to do" (Mark 14:8).

# SEVEN

# TOXICITY OF POWER

*These will be the ways of the king who will reign over you:*
*he will take your sons and appoint them to his chariots and*
*to be his horsemen, and to run before his chariots.*

—1 Samuel 8:11

❧ There is a famous saying: "Power tends to corrupt, and absolute power corrupts absolutely. Great men are almost always bad men."[1] The shortened version, "Power corrupts," is flung about as a response whenever a story of some political, business, or religious leader's unethical or immoral practice is revealed. Power possesses a toxicity. Sometimes someone will send me an essay with headings of some variance that state, "If women ruled the world . . ." It goes on to present some utopian view of women's leadership creating a world of no war, no hungry children, a land or institution of nurture and care for all. Yet we have enough examples of corrupt women in leadership to know any person who knows power, prestige, and success in life is corruptible.

Samuel argues in 1 Samuel 8 with the people of Israel about their desire for a king like others. The central theological issue is the displacement of the Lord God as king with a human substitute. The practical issue raised by Samuel is the corruptible nature of a human king. He tries to warn them away from creating a powerful human leader. The phrase "He will take" is repeated over and over again for eight verses. Samuel reports that this new king will take their sons, daughters, slaves, cattle, and fields. He goes on to say, "He will take one-tenth of your flocks, and you shall be his slaves" (1 Samuel 8:17).

We are a naturally grasping people. Once put into a position of prominence, we easily become addicted to it. A desire to keep this new level of power or increase of our standing can worm its way into our hearts. Hansen refers to this temptation as "ladder-climbing."[2] While he is specifically speaking about pastors, his description can be broadly applied. "They organize their family life around their career. As they consider a move to find a better position, they are only superficially concerned whether the timing is God's, let alone what it means to their family."[3]

When I moved recently, I had a closing chapel with some of my students. We had talked about this particular temptation in class. In the auditorium they had brought in ladders from all over the place. It was a fun way for them to poke at me a bit. It also caused me to pause and check my motivation and spirit regarding the move. Ladder-climbing can be subtle, and all leaders must be on guard against this temptation. The danger of becoming position-hungry is to treat others as simply rungs on the ladder. This creates anger, hurt, loss of trust, and loss of faith, especially when done in the name of Christ.

In Christian circles we cover up those tendencies with smiles and nice words. Yet most of us have firsthand experiences regarding the realities of the corruptible power at work among Christian leaders. Most of us have had some position in which we have experienced power over others. Honest reflection often demands our confession that it is hard to escape the self-serving tendencies within us. Whenever we begin to sense that the pie slices are limited, we want our fair share. And our "fair share" can often be quite large.

We have already discussed the necessity of understanding our inherent power at work. It is equally important to be self-critical in the use of that power. The power of the Resurrection, the power of the Holy Spirit, the power of roles of authority, and the power of race and gender are all important concepts for the Christian leader to understand. Life and Scripture provide examples illustrating power as a negative or positive force. The religious leaders of Jesus' day used their power negatively, ultimately leading to the Crucifixion. Jesus is the prime example of one who uses his or her power positively to transform lives. The complex dynamics of power need to be explored in the Christian context.

Forbes primarily views power as a negative force. She states that "the religion of power is the antithesis of Christianity"[4] She struggles acutely with the abuse of power within the Christian community. Power destroys relationships and therefore destroys both the person utilizing the power and the person over whom power is being exerted. Forbes says that even when the power is used for a holy purpose, it infects the person. It is toxic, she says, and should be rejected by the Christian. "Jesus rejected Satan's temptation to power, choosing instead the path of powerlessness. If God refuses to use power, should we try?"[5]

When serving as a pastor, I began to notice a slow trickle of visitors from a neighboring church. As I engaged them in conversation, I heard repeating stories of hurt and pain. They had all been "chastised and disciplined" by the pastor. One or two stories of discontent would have been taken with a grain of salt, given the dynamics of church relations. The numbers and variety of people who came and shared this common story told me there was cause for deep concern. This pastor's only response to challenging times seemed to be to exert power. If he was displeased with committee attendance, attitude, actions, children's behavior, or words spoken or unspoken, the people had been banned from leadership. Some of these people were able to find healing and transition to our church. Others were deeply hurt and unable to reconnect.

Forbes differentiates power that comes from authority or position from spiritual power. Spiritual power "creates, redeems, transforms, heals, unifies, strengthens, feeds, serves, resurrects, makes whole and communicates."[6] Too often the power utilized in leadership does not manifest any of these properties. Instead, it is a self-serving power used to control, cloaked in spiritualized language. This self-serving motivation does not necessarily mean the person is gaining in financial or positional success.

It can be equally self-serving when the power is used to control institutional change or protect people and institutions the leader favors. The power is focused on manipulation, achievement, and success.

The foundational motivation can often be fear. This fear can be the loss of financial gain, personal sense of esteem, positional status, or change in valued practices. It is not always overt fear. It can be displaced anxiety about the effects of change or when assumed rights and privileges may be taken away. The journey from gaining positions of power to abusing that power can be subtle.

Often these fatal flaws are not recognized until the leadership issues are revealed by a person's moral collapse or in conversation with those who worked closest to them. Utilizing King David's moral failure with Bathsheba, Miller offers warning signs for potential abuse of power:

1. Giving up those disciplines we still demand of underlings.
2. Believing that others owe us whatever use we can make of them.
3. Trying to fix things up rather than make things right.
4. Closing our minds to suggestion that we ourselves could be out of line.
5. Believing that people in our way are expendable.[7]

It is interesting to note each of these "evidences" seems to circle around a person's self-elevation and other devaluation. The power manifested by Christ—the power to which Christians are called—is one that permeates and enables the Christian to live the life of Christ and is a shared power rather than one that is hoarded. Shared power that honors others is distinctly different than the self-promoting power that Forbes describes.

The toxicity of power is a clever poison and often unrecognized. Often, if the person has always been a member of the ruling majority, he or she is clueless as to how much inherent power is at work in his or her life. The findings of a study measuring the ability of people to take the perspective of another confirmed the inability of powerful people to understand the world view and experience of those without power.[8] The authors conclude, "Across four experiments, we found that power was associated with a reduced tendency to comprehend how other individuals see the world, think about the world, and feel about the world."[9]

Studies have consistently shown that where there is disparity in power, the underclass knows and understands much more about the lives and workings of those who have power than those with power know about them. This knowledge is a basic underclass necessity for survival. For those in power, understanding the perspective of others was never necessary and therefore a highly underdeveloped skill.

This limitation creates great difficulty in correctly perceiving power dynamics. Even more pervasive, people with power will be oblivious to the reactions of those without power to their verbal and nonverbal communication. When confronted by misused power dynamics, the response is often defensiveness and denial. In my own leadership there were times when I was confronted by a member of my fellowship with assumptions, remarks, and decisions that were made based on my status and privilege as a Caucasian, middle-income, American woman. I would love to say I was always graceful and quick to learn in response, but that would not be true.

An illustration of that is the controversy in reaction to LifeWay's Vacation Bible School theme for the summer of 2004. "Far Out, Far East Rickshaw Rally: Racing to the Son" was highly criticized as offensive by the Asian-American community and others.[10] The publisher's response was to explain that in the creation process they had consulted missionaries, mission boards, and native Japanese. Various voices continued to voice concern regarding an Asian-themed program that was primarily sold in the United States and did not include Asian-Americans as consultants. The review of the Internet discussion seems to reveal a creative team who had good intent but a limited ability to perceive how an Asian-American might interpret the materials as offensive and dangerous because it perpetuated stereotypes. The responses from LifeWay spokespeople continued to reveal a defensiveness regarding their motives and the difficulty in understanding another's perspective.[11] The potential harm of this is expressed by one critic who said, "When a group of white Americans decide that this is the way Asian culture should be presented, they have effectively used their power to define us—something that only God should do."[12]

There are many stories of groups from the United States going to other countries with the deep desire to be of help but ending up costing the local hosts time and resources. Some of these groups head into their mission work with little understanding of the power dynamics at work in their relationships with the local leaders. One definition of power is "the capacity to influence other people; it emerges from control over valuable resources and the ability to administer rewards and punishments."[13]

There is one place that was a common destination for United States mission teams where the local people had a wall they called "the gringo wall." Rather than asking local leaders and listening to what would be helpful, teams insisted on doing something "practical," "needed," "measurable." In response, the local leadership created a wall these groups happily painted year after year. They went home celebrating their good work.

Groups have built buildings across property lines, insisted on using materials that would quickly break down in the local weather conditions, failed or refused to get local permits—

and the list goes on. The local leaders knew that to deny these groups the kind of work they wanted to do would result in the teams taking their resources elsewhere.

There is also a high cultural value of hospitality that often pushes the local leadership to welcome all willing groups. Letting teams paint and build, even when it was needless or needed to be redone afterward, at least continued the relationship and preserved some hope that resources would eventually reach the priorities of the local team.

Hidden power dynamics are part of many relationships. The controlled resources are not always financial; they can be emotional, psychological, and spiritual in nature as well. To understand how power is abused and misused by us or others, we need to continue to grow in our understanding of emotional health. To every meeting and encounter we attend we bring all of our family systems and histories with us. Our history includes our experiences shaped by race, gender, and socioeconomic background. This can play havoc in the ways we hear each other and react to each other. We have all been in group settings in which the emotional tension of one member overwhelms and reigns over the working environment. This person might not have positional power, but somewhere he or she has learned to use relational power abusively.

The admonition in seminary was for new pastors to discover the informal power structures at work in the church. Some of these informal structures can have merit. It is appropriate for a person whose consistent years of service and wisdom have allowed him or her to become someone whose opinions are considered deeply. However, informal power structures can also be destructive if leaders use their familial relationships, threaten the loss of resources or support, or use their forceful personalities to control others.

Christian groups can be especially vulnerable to this kind of power. In our attempts to be nice, we often let people act in ways that would be considered unacceptable in secular settings. We don't change a program out of concern for the hurt feelings it will cause, even if it would be for the good of the whole. We don't tell a person that his or her outburst was inappropriate, because we are afraid the person might leave. Their actions and these reactions both show a need for emotional growth and healing.

Peter Scazzero leads a dynamic, multicultural, growing church, but he found his leadership was almost his death before he began to discover ways to become emotionally healthy.[14]

He challenges leaders and churches: "Something is desperately wrong with most churches today. We have many people who are passionate for God and his work, yet are unconnected to their own emotions or those around them. The combination is deadly, both for the church and the leaders' personal lives."[15]

This disconnect from our interior lives often means the toxic side of power goes unchecked. A person in leadership must create time for personal reflection on many of the challenges to a healthy emotional life. Reflecting on the power dynamics of his or her home life, the use of power in present relationships, and the meaning of power would all be important exercises to protect himself or herself from the more toxic side of power.

Sanders talks about several perils of leadership in his classic study on Christian leadership.[16] His discussion regarding the leader's temptation of self-pride has important connections to the misuse of power. He provides three questions for the leader to use as a personal review.

How do we react when another is selected for the position we expected to have or wanted to fill?

How do we feel when others identify problems or weaknesses in us?

Does criticism lead to immediate resentment and self-justification?[17]

These questions challenge persons in leadership to consider how important power has become and how it is used as a guard against personal and colleague review.

When I moved from serving as a senior pastor to teaching at a Christian university, I found the loss of power in the local church disorienting. I felt great frustration and angst as I realized that I no longer had the positional power to effect change in my local church. Thankfully, I had a friend going through the same adjustments. We often confessed the mixed emotions we felt due to this loss of power. Some of these adjustments were simply natural job transition issues. Other reactions revealed unhealthy parts of us that had been fed by the power we experienced as pastors in the local church.

I remember early in this transition standing at the back of the sanctuary after the morning worship service and realizing that there was no one interested in my opinions and thoughts, nor did I have any information that was important for others to hear. *I am not significant* flashed through my brain. This reveals so much that was unhealthy in the ways my sense of significance had been fed by positional power.

Healthy introspection is necessary for people in positions of leadership. It is important to understand what motivates action or inaction in certain situations. It is vital to have people we trust and who know us well that can challenge our assumptions.

I appreciate a leader who is able to express charisma, compassion, and has the ability to lead an organization forward. Yet if I discover that the leader, for all his or her good gifts, has no one who can challenge his or her assumptions, speak truth in love regarding his or her verbal and nonverbal communication, I grow increasingly concerned for the ultimate outcomes of the person's leadership. These concerns would be for both the leader's personal life and the life of the institution he or she serves. Everyone is vulnerable to myopic viewpoints and potential abuse of power.

Still, power that comes from position, relationships, or by belonging in the ruling paradigm can be used positively. The leader can recognize the necessity to share this power, creating space for those who do not have power. This will not be done perfectly. There is much for a person who has always had power to learn about the experience of others, and that can be a difficult process.

Often it is the very person who is trying to make personal and systemic change who has also made himself or herself available to hear critiques. This does not feel like much of an award for the person's newly enlightened ways. I have known denominational leaders who have committed themselves to being advocates for women in leadership. This commitment has led to opportunities for close working relationships with women leaders. The relationships have been honest and true, which included receiving critiques regarding language, practices, or systems that are harmful to women. The process of healing for every community who has experienced disproportionate power is important. Any healing and growth process will include uncomfortable and painful moments. Leaders will often not hear the whole perspective of those without power until trust is earned. Depending on how long the history of misused power, no matter how benevolent, this can take a significant amount of time.

It is possible for a person of power to recognize that the systems in which he or she is thriving have significant limitations for others. The combination of a true desire for change and knowledge of how the inside of a system works and positional power can be used for dynamic change.

In one instance I heard of a male leader who recognized the necessity for female leadership. He asked a woman if she was willing to take leadership of a certain committee. When she said she was, he then said, "Watch this." He proceeded to set the stage for her nomination and following vote of affirmation. He knew the system well enough to manipulate it successfully so that securing the position for her was basically a done deal. This committee had previously been run by a man, and these men were chosen in quite the same way. This might not feel particularly fair or right, yet we must admit that there are informal systems in play in choices for leadership roles.

At the same time, it is important to engage in critiques of systems and work toward changes. The hidden processes need to be uncovered and made accessible—to all.

If systemic change is going to happen, it is necessary for someone who has been in power to publicly identify these hidden processes. This leader can utilize his or her inherent power of what this privilege has afforded for the purpose of serving others. Becker's understanding that "power over" is not to be assumed negative is an important balance to Forbes's concerns.[18]

On the other hand, Forbes's caution on the toxicity of power must not be ignored. For power to be used in healthful ways, leaders must have accountability regarding how the power is being potentially used or abused in their lives. This accountability must be given by people who would have different perspectives on the effects and responses to the leaders' verbal and nonverbal communication.

Forbes establishes that power is at play in all relationships.[19] To deny the presence of power in relationships is to leave it unrestrained. Instead, each person must acknowledge the power that is at work in his or her relationships and be cognizant of the multiple manifestations it can take. When leaders recognize their power, they can utilize it for the greater good. This recognition allows people to offer whatever power they have to the glory of God and the service of others.

A white male must recognize the inherent power he will have in many systems and be aware that this same power is not as readily available to women and people of color within the same system. When this inherent power is recognized, potential is created for it to be used in service to others. While the people of the Church may choose to emphasize spiritual power, power at work because of position, role, and the larger sociological systems must be recognized as well.

Power is ultimately necessary for the fulfillment of the mission. In the context of the church, this power is best expressed when the church is galvanized around its sense of mission. Becker names one aspect of power as inner authority, which is an assuredness, an inner strength that is convincing for the leader and others. She gives an example of a Lutheran relief team that was empowered as individuals and a group because of their shared mission. "The sense of common purpose and the sense of urgency in this team combine to give each of the team members as well as the team itself a source of authority that comes from within."[20] This inner conviction overrides personal ambivalences and esteem issues.

A healthy aspect of leadership power is the strength to endure. This endurance is an essential quality for the life of any leader. This resilience includes the absolute faith that the organization or church they serve can fulfill its promise. For Christian leaders, endurance is founded on their relationship to God. When power is bathed by the work of the Holy Spirit, restrained by accountability, and balanced by humility, great leadership can be born. Power that is purified by servanthood can create far-reaching change.

Theologically, this power is evidenced by Jesus on the Cross, making the ultimate sacrifice. "Jesus leads with power. His power to lead finds its ultimate expression not in a throne but in a cross. Jesus' lordship comes to fruition not through domination and coercion but through humility and service."[21] We must hold lightly to positional power. As soon as we begin to grasp it, its toxins are released. We must hold tightly or be tightly held by the power available to us in the name of the Father, Son, and Holy Spirit.

# EIGHT

# NECESSARY BLEND

*Let the same mind be in you that was in Christ Jesus, who, though
he was in the form of God, did not regard equality with God as something
to be exploited, but emptied himself, taking the form of a slave,
being born in human likeness.*
—Philippians 2:5-7

❧ For Christian leaders, power must be blended with humility.
Christ modeled a power that is shown through humility in the
Incarnation, Crucifixion, and Resurrection. Humility protects a
leader from using power in an abusive way and accentuates the
positives of fulfilling a mission. Humility helps the leader celebrate power displayed in the lives of others. Healthy humility
helps the leader value himself or herself and others for deeper
realities than what they do or can achieve.

A Christian leader is particularly called to balance leadership power with humility in light of the incarnation. The model
of Christ continues to inform the Christian leader that servant leadership and humility are the template for their lives.
In Philippians Paul celebrates the humility of Christ as a virtue that ran against common negative perceptions of his time.
Some have wondered if the Greek communities' desire to view
themselves as great limited their willingness to consider a God
whose essence would show how small they really were.[1] The
desire to view their culture as great would also run against the
call to personal humility. The biblical material calls people to
remember a God who is much larger than they and the appropriate humility in response.

Pride, on the other hand, is a wrong focus on oneself. It is love that should rightly be turned to God but is turned inward instead. When people think more of themselves than of God or others, their minds and hearts are closed to receiving important information. In Christian tradition pride is considered a source or evidence of sin. Humility is the correcting virtue to the vice of pride.[2]

Thomas à Kempis draws this parallel as well. When speaking of pride, he says, "Do you believe in yourself? Believe even more in others; this attitude preserves your humility."[3] Thomas Aquinas regarded pride as the desire for exaltation, which was countered by humility, the exalting of God and the presence of God in others.[4] Humility is not portrayed as a degradation of self as much as it is an understanding of God. The call to humility is a call to understand the limitations of humanity and therefore accept the need for grace on behalf of all of humanity when coming before a God who is Creator, infinite and almighty.

The theme of humility in the life of the Christian has been a focus of church leaders and writers across the ages. Benedict of Nursia, Bernard, Abbot of Clairvaux, and Jeremy Taylor were among many who challenged the people of God to take on the humility of Christ.[5] Andrew Murray continues with this emphasis on the essential quality of humility in his book. He says, "Humility is not so much a grace or virtue along with others; it is the root of all, because it alone assumes the right attitude before God and allows Him as God to do all."[6] Murray sees the weakness of the Church as a lack of attention to humility. The Christian life is like a tree, and when humility is not at its root, the whole life system is weakened.

Augustine was a major source for the Church's view of pride and humility. Pride, he said in his confessions, "was one of the chief impediments to loving you and revering you with chaste fear."[7] Instead, what is owed to God is "humble and single-hearted service."[8] J. Patout Burns noted that for Augustine,

"Pride is the root form of evil, separating the self from God and playing itself out in claims to moral self-sufficiency, to religious superiority, and to political domination."[9] Pride is understood to be the major obstacle to overcoming evil. According to Augustine, the antidote is humility. Pride was considered the deadliest of the seven sins; therefore, if humility is the cure, it is of vital importance for the Christian life. Those who embrace Christ and the model of humility will know the power of the resurrection. Those who exalt themselves will know eternal chaos.

Humility was additionally stressed for clergy who, given the privileges often granted to them, could have easily fallen into pride. Lee F. Bacchi notes, "For Augustine, the ordained minister demonstrated humility ontologically by remembering that he, too, was a member of the people of God, a fellow-disciple along with all the other Christian faithful under the one Master Jesus Christ."[10]

In his sermon "Christ in His Mystical Body," Augustine explores the humility of Christ and the invitation for the believer to be changed by that humility, using Matthew 4. When talking about the temptation of Christ, he describes the humility of one who is fully divine being fully human: "For he was hungry, because this too was part of His humiliation. For the bread hungered, the Way was lost, Our Healing was wounded, and Life died."[11]

Augustine interpreted the temptation of Christ to be that of using the power available for purposes other than to glorify God. Humility was seen as the great corrective to abusing power for selfish purposes. Humility expressed in this passage reveals power rather than weakness. If he had given in to the temptation, he may have looked powerful, but the result would have been a loss of power to Satan. Just as love misplaced brings dishonor to God and ultimately leads one to sin, so power misused is an aberration to God. Jesus was the ultimate model of power at its strongest when it is given in service, sacrifice, and humility.

Diane Leclerc's study on the definition of sin in light of women's experience offers nuances when understanding the vice of pride, the virtue of humility, and the concept of sin. She proposes the sin common to women is better described as "relational idolatry."[12] Relational idolatry happens when primary relationships are placed before a person's relationship with God. This has been a common temptation among women, partially because the church affirmed relational idolatry, while not using those words, as an appropriate expression of humility for women. Service to their families was often affirmed as the primary role and only role for Christian women.

Yet Christian women, like all disciples of Christ, are called to put God first. After experiencing a full surrender to God, some women began to sense for the first time that their service to God may include more than serving only their children or extended family.

Issues of pride have not been prevalent in women, while an unhealthy humility would be common. Critical concerns regarding self-esteem among women have been expressed in both academic and popular magazine publications. Leclerc says, "Except for rare exceptions, women have spent centuries suppressed and silenced in the name of Christian humility."[13] Carol Lakey Hess cautions the application of humility to women as well: "When pride is the sin to be overcome and humility is the virtue to achieve, spiritual practices may, unfortunately, become 'steps of ruin for girls and women.'"[14] The sin of self-abnegation needs to have a theological weight in women's lives. Women need to have an independent system of self-definition that reflects a self-understanding of worth and value before embracing an appropriate humility. I have been privileged to see women in small-group settings discover their deep value in God's kingdom. Often this occurs as they study Jesus' relationship of love with women in the gospels. In light of these discoveries many confess a general sense of distance of God that had been based on the notion of being a second-class citizen in God's kingdom.

In Jim Collin's book *Good to Great* he established humility as one of the important characteristics for leaders who can bring organizations to new levels of success.[15] Effective women leaders find it is important to embrace a proper sense of humility. This demands that a woman leader define humility in a larger way then it is often given to her by the church. A proper definition would include words like *affirmation, worth, strength,* and *power,* and not words like *self-degradation* or *abnegation.*

The humility of Christ and the power at work in Christ are key themes in Paul's writings. The kenosis hymn found in Philippians is a prime example.

> Let the same mind be in you that was in Christ Jesus, who though he was in the form of God, did not regard equality with God as something to be exploited, but emptied himself, taking the form of a slave, being born in human likeness. And being found in human form, he humbled himself and became obedient to the point of death—even death on a cross. Therefore God also highly exalted him and gave him the name that is above every name, so that at the name of Jesus every knee should bend, in heaven and on earth and under the earth, and every tongue should confess that Jesus Christ is Lord, to the glory of God the Father (*Philippians 2:5-11*).

This passage has generally been regarded as an early Christian hymn. It serves as an example of humility and love. Verse five serves as a hinge, establishing the preceding characteristics as the right Christian attitude and then pointing to the example of Jesus Christ. Paul builds an argument for unity, which he sees as essential for the church of Philippi to fulfill its calling. This unity is based on self-sacrifice, humility and shared power.

The focus shifts from the dangers of the threatening nature of the world to the threat of a divided community. The power to heal these threats is in the willingness of the Christ follow-ers to come before God and each other in humility. Unity is essential for the fulfillment of the mission and made possible only through authentic humility. This authentic humility em-powers the Christian to value others while also doing the same for himself or herself.

The Philippians are called to humility (*tapeinophrosyne*). Humility then is necessary for the people as individuals and as a church to fulfill the purposes of God in and through their lives. This call was odd for the secular Greek to hear. Humility was seen as the attitude of servility, a person of low birth.[16] Hu-mility would not have been considered a virtue in Greek soci-ety. Markus Bockmuehl says, "In secular Greek it is rarely used, and then in a derogatory sense to denote servile weakness, ob-sequious groveling or on the other hand mean spiritedness".[17]

The Old Testament had a more positive sense of humility. Humility was considered the proper attitude that all people are to have before God. The biblical view of humility was not an in-dication of low self-esteem or a base attitude but rather a mark of moral strength and integrity. Humility involves acknowledg-ment of one's own humanity and a trust in God's power and provision.

My support group of women leaders found ourselves con-sistently encouraging each other to have tough skins and soft hearts. We understood that leadership experiences threatened the healthy state of our hearts. Every leader is in a place of potential attack. A women leader experiences those common "hits" as well as gender-related reactions. We were careful to protect ourselves from a spirit of bitterness and brittleness. We determined to keep ourselves humble before God and with a humble spirit in service to God before others.

A humble or soft heart is open to correction, grace, and love. We continued to discover the necessity of the work of the Holy Spirit and the words of this circle of friends in keeping us in the right state of heart for the leadership roles for which God had called us. This spirit of humility was a daily work of God. ✡

The tough skin part of the call speaks to the empowerment of God to move forward. As pastors, lawyers, advocates, and program directors, we each needed the surrounding protection of God to fulfill the mission to which we were called. We could not fold, because so many depended on us to be true to our call. So while we prayed diligently with each other over the state of our hearts, we also prayed for holy strength and boldness in times of attack. We were each other's sounding boards for times when we needed to speak up against injustice or move forward through times of resistance. To be change agents in our world demanded that we be strong and courageous. We needed God's power to accomplish the calling we had received to lead.

This power is what Paul is addressing in Philippians as he earnestly calls the Church to humility and power. Paul understands that for the community to move forward, it must be in the same mind and heart. This unity of purpose is possible only by the blend of humility and power.

Four appeals are made for this unity beginning with the word "if": "If you have any encouragement from being united with Christ, if any comfort from his love, if any fellowship with the Spirit, if any tenderness and compassion" (Philippians 2:1, NIV). The "if" in the statement does not connote doubt; rather, it expresses a power more than sufficient to accomplish what is being named. The Christian community is reminded of the resources of encouragement and compassion found in the life together in Christ. These verses flesh out key characteristics and experiences for leaders: encouragement, comfort, fellowship with the Spirit, and hearts of tenderness and compassion. The phrase "encouragement [*paraklesis*] in Christ" contains the ideas of consolation and strengthening as in giving someone courage. The phrases "comfort from his love and fellowship" (*koinonia*) "in the Spirit" reveal what Paul understands to be spiritual resources available to create Christian love and unity. This unity of community is created and empowered by the Spirit. The fellowship has its source and origin in Christ. Paul continues to layer his argument. When he speaks of tenderness and compassion, he is appealing to the Philippians to be "in Christ," which will result in a common love for each other.

Paul takes these "if" statements toward the natural conclusion he wants the people to make. If all these resources are available to the people of God (and the assumption is that they are), then the command is to live out those realities. If all these clauses are true, the people have no choice but to be a harmonious, unified people who can therefore fulfill their mission.

Philippians 2:4 is a restatement of the nature of humility: "Each of you should look not only to your own interests, but also to the interests of others" (NIV). Unlike the Roman culture in which the Philippians lived, the new community has a nonhierarchical intent. The leadership and service of the Philippians' community were to be marked by humility. Paul's point is that Christians are called to make an investment into the lives of others without thought of personal gain. This mutuality of love is to be the mark of the Christian community.

The humility of Jesus had a significant influence on the Early Church's notion of humility. As the Christ hymn in Philippians 2:5-11 goes on to demonstrate, true humility is a mark not of weakness but of strength. To be a Christian is fully possible only if Christians are in Christ. In Christ the heart of the Christian is transformed to love others first.

Christ is the model Paul holds before the Philippians' community. Jesus did not think He needed to take advantage of this equality with God; He did not consider it *harpagmos* to be equal to God.[18] In the context of Paul's letter, humility is best understood as the commitment of Christ not to hold on to the advantage of His equality with God. Equality with God was not a matter of receiving or grasping but of giving. Equality with God was not to be selfishly exploited. If Christ, who is equal to God, set aside His own interests for the sake of others, so should Christians.

Philippians 2:7-8 spells out the humility that Christ chose in place of the self-serving attitude rejected in verse six. Rather than grabbing for himself from the advantage of equality, He emptied himself. The verb *keno* can mean to "deprive" or "make of no effect."[19] This is also defined as self-emptying. A kenotic basis for leadership assumes the leader has the larger mission in mind. This characteristic is manifested by a leader's primary passion of fulfilling the purposes and goals of the church or organization. A kenotic basis for relationships is a commitment to be a person who looks out for the well-being of others. Humility and power in a leader allows the leader to empty himself or herself in the service to others as well as to help others see the power they have through God to succeed.

Christ lived as if He were not divine in order to serve humanity in love. The phrase Paul uses here for "humbled himself" signifies the act of placing oneself in solidarity with the humiliated.[20] Hence, this humility is not only the absence of selfishness but also a commitment to others regardless of their positions or prestige.

This choice to be a servant, to display humility, is made evident in the Incarnation and the Crucifixion. The Crucifixion is a deliberate climax to this section. Not only was this humility seen in the willingness of Christ to die but also in the willingness to die shamefully. Christ is, therefore, the example of true humility. Gerald F. Hawthorne describes the breadth of humility portrayed in the life and death of Christ:

True humility is to choose the will of God over one's own will. It is to decide to go God's way rather than one's own way. And in the case of Christ's humility was for him to purpose to radically obey God, even at his own expense, even if it cost him his life to do so, even if he must die by crucifixion![21]

Philippians 2:9 moves from Christ's humility to God's exaltation, which is expressed in the prophetic word that foresees the time when everyone will bow at the name of Jesus. Bockmuehl notes that the exaltation was not the incentive for Christ's acceptance of humility. "Theologically, his exaltation is not a reward but rather a counterbalance to the acceptance of suffering."[22] The promise of exaltation is not the reason given for the Philippians to follow His example of humility. Instead, as F. Bruce says, "[S]ince he was the one whom they now confessed as Lord over all, his example should be decisive for them."[23]

The conclusion drawn from this hymn, as Paul has used it, is a call to humility, love, unity, and service. This call is built on nothing less than the paradigm Jesus had lived before them. The rhythms of discipleship can be heard: the greatest must be the servant; to gain life it must be lost; to receive, a person must release.

Ultimately, true power is displayed in humility. The power to fulfill this call is found in a life of humility before God and in service to others. The alternative message of the world encourages people to grab any territory or rights they can, to self-promote, and to self-protect. Paul calls the Philippians away from those characteristics so they might know the beauty of living in community with others who have the mind of Christ. Christians are called to be a people who have the blend of humility and power at work in their lives.

Our willingness to be humbled is never to be confused with humiliation. Nor does it express some sort of weakness or inability to accomplish goals or lead organizations. Christlike humility still allows one to have a sense of worth and value. A person of humility is able to speak forcefully with conviction while not attempting to overpower with dominance. A holistic, biblical understanding of humility is essential.

In Collins's work, a primary characteristic of the highest leadership level was a blend of personal humility and professional will.[24] Discovery of this characteristic was not by self-deprecating comments; these leaders rarely talked about themselves negatively or positively. At the same time, they expressed a dogged determination to lead their businesses to greatness. As women leaders God calls us to use our gifts and graces. We also know that not all people within our church communities will be supportive of those calls. Hence, the necessity for persistence in the face of injustice, accusation, and outright attack are essential.

The leaders in Collins' study didn't seek to turn the center of attention on themselves but rather to keep the attention on the larger goal of building a great company. The leaders had a strong belief in the company's ability to achieve greatness and had a ferocious resolve to do whatever was necessary to make the company great, including a willingness to make sacrifices, tough decisions, and look with brutal honesty at both functional and dysfunctional realities. Part of this brutal honesty takes place when women in leadership name both their gifts and obstacles.

One of my friends worked with the state legislature for the advocacy of childcare. She was often weary from the battle. In the times of prayer and listening, a spark was often reignited as she talked about her sense of calling. Her passion for the importance of advocating for these children, and the vision to see the possibility of public and private sectors working together, helped her move forward one step at a time. Every victory was celebrated in our small group. She was always quick to talk about the significant work of others in her office and the partnerships they were forging. But when you stood back, you could see the necessity of her quiet, determined leadership in ultimately achieving the goal.

The themes of humility and power arise throughout Philippians. A key verse is "I want to know Christ and the power of his resurrection and the sharing of his sufferings by becoming like him in his death, if somehow I may attain the resurrection from the dead" (Philippians 3:10-11).

Humility and power can be found throughout the second and third chapters of Philippians. Philippians 2:3-4 says, "Do nothing out of selfish ambition or vain conceit, but in humility consider others better than yourselves. Each of you should look not only to your own interests, but also to the interests of others" (NIV).

Philippians 2 and 3 emphasize the qualities of personal sacrifice, diligent commitment, and brutal honesty combined with unfailing hope. Paul speaks clearly about the realities facing these early believers, and in these chapters he specifically addresses the obstacles for Timothy and Epaphroditus (Timothy's readiness to travel and Epaphroditus' homesickness and illness).

A case in point of unfailing hope that leads to resolve is found when Paul says, "Not that I have already obtained all this, or have already been made perfect, but I press on to take hold of that for which Christ Jesus took hold of me" (Philippians 3:12, NIV). This verse reveals a persistent will that through the power of God at work in believers will enable them to fulfill their missions in life.

Perhaps the greatest scriptural expression of hope is found in Philippians 4:13—"I can do all things through Christ who strengthens me" (NKJV). This statement follows a series of exhortations that he gives the Philippians that they might stay true to God and committed to their missions. This hope is based on a trust that God is able to provide the power for Christians to fulfill the call of God on their lives. For the pastor-leader, the greatest professional will is a will based on faith in God.

Humility is not an adjective often used for Paul. Nevertheless, it is appropriate within this discussion. While he expresses a strong sense of himself and his gifts, Paul never puts himself forward as the primary concern. Over and over again he emphasizes the importance of Christ being first and foremost in the life of the Church. Marty Wooten's study of 2 Corinthians establishes Paul's servant heart:

Paul is making the point that in preaching his message he is not promoting himself and making himself out to be the standard. By holding up Jesus Christ as Lord, he was in reality serving the Corinthians and not enforcing his own authority.[25]

Paul clearly knew his personal strengths. He did not deny his intelligence, discipline, or heritage. When he boasted, it was about what Christ did in his weakness. He also made clear throughout his letters that no hierarchy exists among believers. In his letter to the Galatians he says, "There is neither Jew nor Greek, slave nor free, male nor female, for you are all one in Christ Jesus" (Galatians 3:28, NIV). He approaches with power and humility each of the situations in the churches to which he writes. He does not shirk from confronting the concerns he has for the community. His motivation to confront is the desire for reconciliation between people and God. He is the first to admit he was one of the greatest of sinners, he did not deserve the love of God, and he had weaknesses. When writing to the Corinthians, he says, "I am the least of the apostles and do not even deserve to be called an apostle, because I persecuted the church of God" (1 Corinthians 15:9, NIV).

In Paul's letter to the Philippians, this humility comes through during a time of great opposition in his ministry as he waits for judgment from the courts. This waiting period would have been difficult even in the midst of Paul's assurance regarding death and life both being for the glory of God. In addition, while he was imprisoned, some detractors questioned his leadership and made malicious remarks against him. His response to this challenge is found in Philippians:

Some proclaim Christ from envy and rivalry, but others from goodwill. These proclaim Christ out of love, knowing that I have been put here for the defense of the gospel; the others proclaim Christ out of selfish ambition, not sincerely but intending to increase my suffering in my imprisonment. What does it matter? Just this, that Christ is proclaimed in every way, whether out of false motives or true; and in that I rejoice *(Philippians 1:15-18)*.

In a time of great suffering, Paul had good cause to make an argument on his own behalf. He had every reason to call those who support him to attack those who preach for malicious reasons and attack his name. His reputation, ministry, and integrity are on the line. Even in times like these, Paul is focused on Christ and on the mission of proclaiming Christ. He would not call the Early Church to become embroiled in a controversy over him but rather insisted they stay focused on the mission and Christ alone.

The leader's basis for that hope is founded on the model of the incarnation as well as the power of the Resurrection at work in every believer's life. The life and death of Jesus Christ are the ultimate models of power and humility. The implications of the incarnation upon the Christian's life are important to investigate.

This humility in the midst of power is the inexplicable character of God expressed in the incarnation. The thought that a God who created all things, who always is and always was, would have any interest in humanity, let alone any one particular member of humanity, is difficult to fathom. Nevertheless, the incarnation fully reveals this God who comes and dwells with us and has relationship with humanity. Bervard S. Childs points out that the incarnation is a revelation of the character of Christ. He states, "Jesus' incarnation was not an isolated event at the beginning, but his whole life is portrayed as one of submission to the will of God, even unto death."[26] The God who comes down and is seen throughout the Scriptures and most significantly in the incarnation of Jesus Christ. Jesus, who was fully God, was willing to take on the limitations of the human existence. He who had no needs entered into a world in which he would have needs that would create a dependence on others. "In other words, the incarnation involved God's subjecting himself to the limitations of humanity in order to achieve his purposes of revelation and reconciliation."[27]

In Christ, God's character is revealed in a blend of humility and power. Through entering Christ's humility, the people of God can know the power of God at work in and through their lives. The practice of humility will empower the Church to fulfill the mission. As church leaders seek to reflect the image of God, this combination of humility and power becomes an important combination of qualities for leadership.

# NINE

# SERVANT LEADER

*During supper Jesus, knowing that the Father had given all things into his hands, and that he had come from God and was going to God, got up from the table, took off his outer robe, and tied a towel around himself.*
—John 13:3

⁓❧⁓❧

⁓❧ We have heard quite a bit in the last few years about the call to be servant leaders. Greenleaf first introduced the phrase "servant leader" to common usage among business leaders in the 1970s.[1] These themes were not explored because of an overt religious commitment. Instead, themes arose from his study of leaders who cast a vision larger than personal success. The inclusion of the community good as a leadership value was a significant contribution from Greenleaf.

Collins, in his work published thirty years later, discovered the importance of similar values. He avoided the language of servant leadership, because his research team did not think it held in tension the predominate characteristics of humility and professional will. Collins was specifically uncomfortable with the word *servant*. His research team convinced him that calling the Level Five leaders *servants* or *servant leaders* sounded weak or meek.[2] They believed strongly that the label would overstress humility.[3] This discomfort is founded in the ongoing assumption that humility lacks power to effectively achieve mission. Again, we see quite the opposite in Christ. Despite Collins' resistance to using the language of servant leadership, he was able to affirm the importance of the combination he preferred to describe as "humility with professional will."

A servant leader is understood as one who serves others in a way that empowers them to function better than they otherwise would. They emphasize the importance of other people's highest good being served rather than personal gain or expression of power. A servant leader does not insist on being the center of attention. At its best, servant leadership is an expression of the love leaders have for their people and the larger community.

Greenleaf particularly looked at the importance of life significance and community responsibility. Greenleaf encouraged leaders to see the greater gain realized when the core values of servant leadership are enacted by individuals and institutions. Greenleaf's description of a servant leader is expressed through questions:

> Do those being served grow as persons: do they, while being served, become healthier, wiser, freer, more autonomous, more likely themselves to become servants? *And* [original emphasis] what is the effect on the least privileged in society; will she or he benefit, or, at least, be not further deprived?

He adds a further stipulation which is:

> No one will knowingly be hurt by the action, *directly or indirectly* [original emphasis].[4]

Greenleaf says a servant leader is a servant first. Other people's highest good being served is more important than personal gain or any expression of power. This type of leader creates an atmosphere of growth and achievement. Servant leadership emphasizes a combination of teamwork and community, personal involvement in decision-making, and ethical and caring behavior.

Servant leaders have honed their ability to listen well. Servant leaders make no assumptions of knowing everything; neither are they threatened by the good ideas of others. A commitment to active, humble listening creates a leader who is more able to hear from the community. This leader, through listening, can successfully produce a cohesive creation from the ideas that emerge.

Servant leaders are not ambitious for themselves but for the general success of stated goals. An ambition that focuses on the broader goals increases the trust people will have in the leader. In this atmosphere people can trust that space will be given for all to grow and realize significance in their shared mission. The word *ambition* comes from a Latin word meaning "campaigning for promotion."[5] Effective leaders have a level of ambition within their character. These leaders do desire to be successful. The significant difference is that the focus does not remain myopically on their personal achievements. A servant leader's task is to submit personal ambition under the larger goals.

A Christian who is a servant leader needs to be marked by an ambition to achieve the true character of God's kingdom. The Christian leader often struggles with the tension between the desire to serve and glorify God along with a desire to succeed. Ongoing conflict over motive and ambition can be disturbing for the leader who truly desires to be a servant of God. Sanders says, "Ambition that centers on the glory of God and welfare of the church is a mighty force for good."[6] This kind of ambition, when bathed consistently in prayer, is an important characteristic for a leader who desires to dream dreams and see visions come to reality.

Long before Greenleaf or Collins wrestled with the concept of servant leadership, Jesus lived, breathed, and taught it. Jesus established the concept of greatness in God's kingdom coming through service. This language of servanthood has been at times misused in the history of the Church. Leaders have portrayed a false humility and claimed to be servants of all when they were clearly servants of none. Almost all church systems could name such a leader as well as the well-known fall of the televangelist. On the other hand, others have served with true humility. These leaders modeled through their actions and spirit that they had embraced the call to be the incarnation of God's presence in the world through humility and power.

Mother Teresa was a well-known example. She served the poor for most of her life on the streets of India. She also founded the Missionaries of Charity, which serves the poorest of the poor around the world. Many relatively unknown people have lived out this kind of servant leadership establishing missions, churches, hospitals, schools, and clinics around the world.

Sanders describes one of the essential characteristics of one of the first missionary leaders to India, Adoniram Judson, as "self-reliance balanced by humility."[7] Leaders have natural gifts that are seen as given by God. These gifts can be used to serve self or others. There is a powerful spiritual leadership that arises when leader's personalities are "irradiated, penetrated and empowered by the Holy Spirit."[8]

Prayer is a sign of a seeking heart, and a seeking heart embraces appropriate humility. Prayerful leaders will not forget to whom their lives are owed, from whom all power flows, and through whom life is lived. Prayer also creates the quiet in which the leader can hear from God, know God, and live in obedience to God. This willingness to withdraw gives the servant leader opportunities for renewed perspective that can be lost in daily management tasks.

This does not mean perfect leaders are created. They are humans with personalities, strengths, and weaknesses. In the early 1980s I encountered a woman who stood about four foot eleven, full of personality and ideas. She sensed God calling her to respond to the needs of people in her community. With limited resources, she responded with what she had: her home phone number and her home. As she began to see the need for a larger response, a servant leader was born. The Spirit-filled woman—also known for being stubborn, persistent, insistent, dramatic, and sometimes troublesome—was able to galvanize churches, social services, and town governments to establish feeding programs, a referral center, and a shelter for women and children.

This kind of leader understands that good ideas and answers can originate outside of himself or herself. Sanders points out that every leader is going to face criticism, and the true test of a leader's humility is his or her reaction to those critiques. If in arrogance leaders begin to dismiss feedback, whether positive or negative, they will miss hearing some important words of correction, direction, and vision.

The Blackabys call the servant leader model the strongest Christian influence on leadership both in secular and religious organizations.[9] This work indicates that the primary characteristic of servant leadership is when "leadership flows from the love leaders have for their people."[10] The emphasis on love sounds strikingly familiar to Greenleaf's stress on servant leaders offering acceptance to their employees. He says, "The servant as leader always empathizes, always accepts the person but sometimes refuses to accept some of the person's effort or performance as good enough."[11] Love is what drives a servant leader to look for the higher good rather than personal gain.

Humility is what keeps this love and nurture from becoming overly paternalistic or maternalistic. The servant leader values people, cares for them, and also understands them as gifted and able. This love creates an atmosphere of trust for those who follow as they understand the leader is not focused on building a personal kingdom. When the leader acts out of personal knowledge of God's love and a desire to love others, the team is energized, for they are not working for some personal, vicarious dream but for something bigger and more meaningful.

This love, therefore, demands an interest in encouraging people to grow and become what God has created them to be. Servant leaders who love will invest in the lives of those who work with them, even if this means these people will grow to a skill level that causes the leader to lose their service in his or her area of work. Servant leaders encourage the professional development of their workers while working with those who are in the wrong jobs and underachieving. They will also be concerned that their workers' lives remain balanced and healthy.

Ultimately Christian leaders must also know whom they serve. In understanding the call to servant leadership, church leaders know they are God's servants. The Blackabys reflect on the illustration of Jesus washing the feet of the disciples, which is often used to exemplify servant leadership. They think it is a vital depiction that is balanced when the reader remembers that Jesus did not wash the disciples' feet every night. Jesus did not become their servant but rather God's servant, who then serves the people around him to God's glory. Hence, the acts of service would be God-inspired. Servant leaders are submitted to God and are following His will and direction. When the service is offered to God in obedience to His call, they are free from seeking appreciation and able to offer themselves in love and with joy.

R. Paul Stevens addresses the importance of serving God over others:

> This concept of the servant of the Lord is radically different from the contemporary view of ministry which boils down to being servants of people or the church for God's sake rather than serving God for the benefit of people and God's world. The difference is subtle and sublime. The essence of ministry/service is being put at the disposal of God. The need is not the call to service. The call comes from God.[12] The servant is God's servant, pure and simple.

This subtle shift is invaluable for the pastor's or leader's emotional and mental health as he or she offers himself or herself in humility to the service of God. Servant leaders function with an understanding that this power arises from a dependence upon God. This humility creates leaders in secular and religious institutions who are able to see the larger picture. Such leaders can be honest about the present obstacles and therefore are more likely to offer trustworthy leadership.

Greenleaf believes the trustworthiness of the servant leader is increased when he or she cares for those in the organization:

> Servant-leaders are functionally superior because they are closer to the ground—they hear things, see things, know things, and their intuitive insight is exceptional. Because of this they are dependable and trusted, they know the meaning of the line from Shakespeare's sonnet: "They that have power to hurt and will do none."[13]

Young's understanding of servant leadership for the Christian is to be a person who seeks first and foremost, with humility, God's leading. From this basis, then, Young proposes the servant leader calls forth the gifts, thoughts, and strengths of others. The servant leader is committed to serving others and equipping and releasing them to become servant leaders as well.[14]

In a study of power in leadership, Thomas Hawkins thinks the only guard against misuse and abuse of power is servanthood.[15] "The key to faithful leadership does not lie in focusing overly on one way of leading with power. It resides in understanding how service and servanthood transform all expressions of leading with power into genuine leadership."[16]

Women leaders and authors have grappled with the language used in a servant leader model. Women experience negative and positive ramifications to their leadership as they seek to understand and implement a biblical model of servant leadership. The role of "servant" has at times been embraced by women while no avenue for leadership or power has been made available in their lives. They have been encouraged to serve in the nursery, kitchen, or children's ministries but not invited to serve in areas that would connote significant leadership and decision making. Successful businesswomen become frustrated when their churches refuse to use their skill even when the need is sorely evident.

Definitions of words such as *servant, humility,* and *power* need to be constantly refined. Culture, through common usage, can quickly misconstrue the meanings. When service, humility, and servanthood are demanded from others (as many women have experienced), the words begin to carry domineering and controlling meanings that were not in the original intent. For example, a woman can be told that she is not showing humility if she likes how she looks, feels good about herself, or voices a differing opinion. Generally, when men are called to be people of service and humility, the life applications are not as limiting. The connotation of these words are skewed when used in isolation. When humility is not balanced with the call to know God's power and esteem, the result can be a misshapen life.

Women leaders have to find new ways of understanding what a servant leader model means for them. Servanthood has often been misapplied and used as a mechanism of control. Male roles in the church have always included the idea of being a servant through leading, speaking, and preaching. Predominant female roles have not included these public forums of service. Words such as *submission, humility,* and *service* all have to be placed in the larger understanding of the woman being a valuable equal who is called to leadership and service. When a healthy concept and contextual respect occurs, a woman in leadership can embrace servant leadership as a viable, healthy, and biblical model.

The strength of this model for women is found in the emphasis upon service and relationships. The correlation of a women's high value of relationship with the values taught with servant leadership are an attractive match. Rather than rest on personal accolades, the strong relational skills of women cause them to search for deeper meaning and connection. In two anthologies produced by the Greenleaf Center for Servant Leadership, articles were written by several women regarding the value of the servant leader model in their roles as leaders.[17] One woman is quoted as saying, "So-called (service-oriented) feminine characteristics are exactly those which are consonant with the very best qualities of servant-leadership"[18]

Frankel describes herself as a "staunch believer" in Green-leaf's servant leadership, but she also thinks that some women can take the outward emphasis to extremes that undermine their ability to lead.[19] She gives an example of a manager who was so busy serving the people on her team that she was not providing the leadership the group needed.

In her book *Leading Women*, Becker looks at, among other things, women's relationships with service and power. She describes the ease with which women often accept "helper roles" to the detriment of their advancement. She points out that women's propensity to function in servant roles has created situations in which they do not fully utilize or recognize their own personal power.[20] If women embrace the humility of servanthood without a sense of professional will or power, they will not accomplish their own goals nor lead an organization into greatness. Becker describes women's struggle with power: "We have trouble knowing and accepting our own power, because we often can't distinguish between healthy, productive power and abusive control."[21]

We are all aware of leaders who have used their positions for personal gain to the detriment of those with whom they worked and the larger community. A person who has suffered under this type of leadership may have a difficult time entertaining the notion that a servant leadership that includes power or passion is possible. In addition, women have had limited access to power and authority, which decreases access to female models of servant leadership. A woman in leadership must find healthy models of women servant leaders who embrace power and authority as part of their lives.

An important aspect of this journey is a full acceptance of her worth as a woman made in the image of God. Sumner explores the effects of church history and the teachings of people like Tertullian, Ambrose, and Augustine regarding notions such as original sin, the image of God, and the culpability of women. These teachings tend to place significant blame on Eve for the fall and limit the scope of a woman being created in the full image of God. Women have unknowingly absorbed an understanding of lower status for their gender. This lower sense of worth affects their ability to lead and to allow other women to lead.[22]

Women leaders often must first acknowledge a renewed sense of self-worth, their creation in the image of God, and their inherent dignity before becoming comfortable with accepting and exerting any power or authority, let alone support other women in leadership.

The complexity of issues surrounding power has caused some women leaders to assume an indirect power. They can lean on their strong relational skills and use them in manipulative ways as they seek a circuitous path to power. The shift into healthier leadership demands a different style.

Rather than using manipulation to get her way, the adult woman must learn to speak with authority, establish boundaries, and develop a healthy understanding of self. This obviously does not mean she gets her own way every time. Instead, this leadership demands real discussion over ideas, philosophy, implications, and ultimately a practice of mutual submission with other decision-makers.

Women particularly have a struggle with authoritative power or "power over" others. The language of power can often take on negative connotations. Becker explores the complex responses a woman leader has to power: "We misinterpret it, fear it, covet it, need it, and at the same time reject it, or at best hold it at a safe distance."[23] Becker describes different ways in which power is manifest as "power over," "power within," and "power with."[24]

"Power over" is generally understood as the authority one has in a hierarchical setting. "Power within" is the recognition of power within a person's inner strength and assurance. "Power with" is the strength available in a web of relationships. In her later work, she renames these as "authoritative power," "charismatic power," and "coactive power."[25] Becker says that each of these forms is legitimate.

Most women embrace the relationally based "power with" model. Women need not reject the different kinds of power, only the abuse of those powers. Becker expresses the problem for women in leadership well:

> In our effort to avoid any use of power that has histori-
> cally abused us, we may indeed fall into a trap: "A kind of
> personal, structureless politics; widespread opposition to
> leader of any kind; an insistence on working collectively;
> and an emphasis on process, often to the exclusion of get-
> ting things done."[26]

In other words, the discomfort and difficulty with accepting power affects women's ability to lead an organization in fulfilling its mission. Women instead need to recognize the power they do have and wield whether consciously or unconsciously. A woman leader needs to become comfortable with a level of personal and professional power that is inherent in her life and professional position. The challenge is to utilize this power for the overall good while avoiding the abusive elements of power.

Servant leaders have to revise standards of success and power in the light of the Cross itself as they seek to minister. Bennet Sims defines servanthood as "neither dominance nor servility. Instead, it is the most enduring form of power, because it is congruent with the relational way things work in the ongoing life of the universe."[27]

In humility, the servant leader recognizes God's power is what empowers the Church (the people of God) to transform the world. The humility of a servant leader is not groveling— it is a commitment to put God and others first. The notion of a God who would choose the way of the Cross to communicate and transform continues to be countercultural even for the Church. Like the Israelites, the Church would often prefer a king who comes with power to subjugate and put all things in order. Instead, God comes and turns everything inside out through His transformative power. The call to servanthood is seen in the nation of Israel, through the life of Jesus and the Early Church.[28]

A thorough study of the Scriptures that speak about servanthood is beyond our scope; however, a few examples are the four servant songs found in Isaiah, Jesus' redefining greatness, in Matthew 20:27-28 and Mathew 23:11, and the passage describing Jesus' washing the feet of the disciples found in John 13:3-17.

Various leaders whose stories are found in the Scriptures were described as servants. Moses is described in terms of humility and service. The references to Moses by God in the Scriptures designate him as "my servant, Moses" (Numbers 12:6-8). Joshua is referred to as "the servant of the Lord" (Joshua 24:29). In Numbers 12:3 Moses is described as "very humble, more than any man who was on the face of the earth." Paul was also self-designated a servant, and he proclaimed a theology of service.

Jesus is the model of servanthood. His is an ongoing commitment to loving friend and foe. His willingness to make sacrifices throughout His life, all the way to death on the Cross, is unprecedented. He caused great distress among the religious leaders as He included the excluded in His community. His prayer was for His followers to share in the intimacy He knew with God the Father. His prayers included forgiveness for those who tortured and killed Him. The example of Jesus continues to underline the blend of humility and power.

Leadership, especially when informed by servanthood, involves suffering. As much as the incarnation continues to scandalize, the Cross continues to shock. Somehow, many servant leaders in the Church assume the Cross and the way of suffering are not to be part of the victorious Christian's life. Nevertheless, when times of suffering come, a larger model in Christ provides a paradigm for understanding suffering. The model of Christ tells us that suffering is a legitimate part of the servant leader's life. The story of the Cross, which includes the Resurrection, helps the servant leader embrace a larger meaning for his or her times of suffering. The passion story helps the suffering servant know "such suffering love cannot be defeated in God's cosmic design."[29]

The Christian leader is a servant. In a study of qualities among successful women pastors, I found they did not hesitate to figuratively wash the feet of the disciples. On the other hand, their servant hearts did not negate their understanding of the power and authority inherent in their leadership roles.

When Jesus entered the world as a suffering servant, He was never a victim of the powers of the world but was instead a power combined with humility that would transform the world. A service of humility that has the power to transform has implications for Christ followers as they seek to live out the call to be servant leaders. Servanthood is made evident as Jesus loved people before any kind of life change had ever happened. He loved those who betrayed Him. He cried, He laughed, He challenged, He listened, and He was patient with those who did not get His message or understand who He was. He who was fully God never considered any person beneath His attention, touch, or love. The incarnation teaches the importance of not grasping after what is understood as a right or due status. Servant leaders know that serving God with humility allows the power of God to work in them and through them.

# TEN

# WOMEN'S WAYS OF LEADING

*Then Mary said, "Here am I, the servant of the Lord;*
*let it be with me according to your word."*
—Luke 1:38

❧❧❧

❧ Women in leadership have often fought the notion of being different. Being different was viewed negatively largely because men have been considered the norm; therefore being "unlike" means to be less than normal. The underlying assumption that women's ways of leading fall outside of what is considered "normal" can create gaps in cross-gender working relationships. Women can be perceived as dangerous or difficult by the fact that they are what Becker calls the "unknown other."[1]

Any differences between men and women noted were often used as reasons women should not lead or why they have not risen to leadership. Leadership assessment should be based on outcomes. Instead, as Becker points out: "We judge women competent or incompetent leaders based on the prevailing models of leadership."[2]

In some ways women are still emerging as they find a greater sense of self and voice from which to speak. Gilligan's seminal work, *In a Different Voice,* is a breakthrough study that looks at distinctive ways women experienced and spoke about moral problems, development. and relationships.[3] Mary Field Belenky and coauthors represent a significant shift in thought as they explored how women develop and learn differently. An ongoing debate exists regarding what aspects of those differences are socially formed or are the essence of being a woman. These authors were not arguing for an essential difference but rather a unique perspective that arises from women's experience.[4] In their later book they clarified their position:

> Although many people have interpreted our work as arguing for essential gender differences, we did not claim that the five perspectives or ways of knowing that we described were distinctly female. We believed that those categories might be expanded or modified with the inclusion of a more culturally and socioeconomically diverse sample and men.[5]

The distinct information is revealed when women's voices are heard, but this does not mean that information is confined to women's experience. Rather, it largely reflects human experience uncovered unless women are included in the focus of a study. In the original study, Belenky and her coauthors talk about five perspectives of knowing: silence, received knowing, subjective knowing, procedural knowing (separate and connected), and constructed knowing.[6]

Women often experience a devaluation of their ways of knowing, learning, and leading when they do not fit into the forms of the common higher educational systems largely structured and taught by white males. The information that women have to offer has often been devalued, increasing their silence.

A knowledge base expressed by many women is experienced, named, and confirmed within a network of relationships. The emphasis on relationships can be a strength *and* weakness for women. Women leaders who maintain strong relationships with colleagues, co-workers, or congregation members find that this network of relationships gives them energy and purpose. These connections both provide support as well as insights into the interpersonal dynamics in the workplace. This web of associations gives them strength as leaders. They often describe their leadership in forms of networks and centers of movement rather than a hierarchical system.

The weakness of this dynamic is evident when the complications of relationships can overcome the work that needs to be done. A study by Karen Lee Ashcraft and Michael E. Pacanowsky, done at a business that employed mostly women, shows ways in which the employees' interpersonal relationships created indirect competition and resistance to direct confrontation.[7]

These practices can undermine the success of the organization. The women employees were generally harsh in their critiques of the gendered quality of the workplace. The study also illuminated ways in which women participate in the devaluation of women. The strong relational aspects of women can hinder the appropriate focus on successfully completing the goal. In addition, too much emphasis on relationships may hinder women leaders from making the tough calls that have relational cost but mission gain.

Conversely, some women function in relative isolation. They may have risen in a knowledge system and worked in institutions that assume a hierarchical male paradigm. In order to survive, they adjusted themselves in ways that were necessary to excel in that system. Their success in these systems may cause them to judge other women harshly who have not been able or were unwilling to make those same adjustments. These women can accept the myth that they are somehow unique from other women; therefore, their leadership leaves them in even greater isolation. They at times will receive accolades from their male counterparts for being "unlike" other women, which is meant as a statement of affirmation.

Some of these women may experience a loss of female identity and community in the midst of their professional development.[8] I have been told many times that I think like a man. Without much reflection, I initially took this statement as a positive affirmation of my abilities. Over time I realized that the statement was also saying something about my femininity and was a clearly negative assessment of a woman's ability to think. I realized some of my moments as the first woman to do or participate in various levels of leadership was not necessarily breaking a barrier. Rather, the system for complex layers of reasons had simply opened the door just for me.

Women leaders who have experienced success and achievement in an otherwise relatively closed system must be careful. They can assume the doors that opened for them are open for other women. I have heard successful women dismiss other women's stories of obstructions and obstacles as insignificant or untrue since that had not been their exeperience. In whatever system we find ourselves working, it is essential for women to continue to advocate for those who face great barriers.

The desired outcome is not simply to throw out one system of leadership for another. With healthy teamwork across gender lines, differences are valued, not erased. Mutual respect is better than assuming one way of effectively doing leadership. Space needs to be created for different models of leadership and ministry. Becker concludes that believing in women leaders does not exclude valuing men's perspectives. "Finally, our criteria for effective leadership in the church would value relationships, inclusiveness, participation and flexibility as much as order, achievement, and power."[9]

In Deborah Tannen's research of women's and men's ways of communicating, significant indicators led to the conclusion that men and women do not communicate alike.[10] Tannen concludes that the goal of conversation is different for men and women. For men, the goal is power; for women, the goal is building relationships. Research seems to suggest that men and women both take men more seriously. Women's ideas are judged more harshly. Women often include a tag line that seems to lessen the authoritative tone of the message.[11] These tag lines, which come across as questions or disclaimers, are often meant to invite the listener to consider the point being made but may instead cast an air of uncertainty.

Examples of tag lines are phrases such as, "Isn't it?" "Don't you know?" "Do you agree?" or "Have you ever experienced . . . ?" Women who adopt a style that does not use these tag lines, which is received as appropriate leadership language from men, can be criticized for their aggressive style. On the other hand, others have noted the positive aspects of tag lines. The phrases may cause a loss in authoritative tone but create a gain in effective communication. Leonora Tubbs Tisdale argues for the positive aspects of this communication style: "There is something highly appropriate—not only communicationally but also theologically—about using speech that creates equality, includes others, and invites rather than demands a response—especially when preaching a gospel that does the same."[12]

Concerns arising from these dynamics are not easily remedied. If a woman is not forceful enough, she is judged weak. If she is too forceful, she is considered masculine and aggressive.

Judgments made against women speakers were reflected in a recent conversation I had with some male colleagues about a woman speaker whom they initially did not receive well. They described her as "striding out on the platform in her Hillary Clinton suit." Only when she shared something of her journey and vulnerability were they willing to listen to what she had to say. Tannen explores these dynamics at great lengths:

Ways of talking associated with masculinity are also associated with leadership and authority. But ways of talking that are considered feminine are not. Whatever a man does to enhance his authority also enhances his masculinity. But if a woman adapts her style to a position of authority that she has achieved or to which she aspires, she risks compromising her femininity in the eyes of others.[13]

This language difference is made evident in how people speak. The types of words used by men and women as well as words used to describe men and women are dissimilar. All these subtle differences affect perceptions of leadership qualities and abilities. For example, you will rarely hear of a nagging husband or a feisty man.

Tannen does not hold one way of communicating to be correct but does stress the importance of having cross-gender understanding so that greater communication can occur. A woman in leadership has to have some competency regarding communicating in such a way that engenders trust in her ability to lead. Ideally that would require adjustments from men and women in their interpretations of communication styles.

In Lois P. Frankel's work as a business consultant, she discovered there were ways in which women communicated and functioned that worked for them in the lower levels of management but created obstacles for further advancement. She coached women to try new behaviors that include different ways of communicating as well as different ways of functioning as a leader. She believes that women often have to make the important transition from being doers to being leaders.[14] Her emphasis was on leading as a woman not as a "girl." When using the term *girl* she is referring to certain attitudes, communication styles, and actions that give an immature presentation rather than one fitting a confident woman leader.

One example she gives is the propensity for women to sit on one foot while in a meeting, which may be cute and even comfortable, but the posture undermines their authority. I still catch myself sitting around a board table and occasionally sitting in a way that may lessen my authoritative presence. This isn't a hard-and-fast rule, but basic awareness of how others might perceive body language, especially in initiatory meetings, is important to take into consideration.

When a study is focused on women in leadership, common elements with their male colleagues are displayed. In addition, unique qualities do arise. Helgesen sought to discover the actual practices of women managers through what she called diary studies. She shadowed women business leaders taking note of significant events, decisions made, meetings, basic schedules, and styles of interaction.

Distinctive leadership practices were discovered by Helgesen when she compared her findings to a similar study with male subjects. The women did not view unscheduled tasks and encounters as interruptions. Secretaries were not used as protectors of their time. The women were more diverse in their associations and activities outside of work.[15]

All of these characteristics underline a high value of people and relationships. These women often viewed themselves as in the center of things rather than at the top.[16] Their authority came from connection to people around them rather than distance from those below. A pattern seemed to emerge that revealed women managers functioning as leaders while staying connected with their coworkers as well as their home lives. Words that were commonly used by these leaders were *flow, interaction, access, conduit, involvement, network,* and *reach.*[17]

The theme of relationships continues to arise in the studies of women. Women generally have a care and concern for others. Whether highly valuing relationships is a gender quality or socialized character is still under debate. This emphasis on relationships and centrist rather than hierarchical leadership may also be a result of what is demanded of a woman in leadership. In a study done by the Center for Values Research, coworkers were less tolerant of women in leadership who lacked human relations skills.[18] Women, as a rule, are not excused for behaviors and poor social skills that are accepted in male counterparts. This study found that women who are successful in leadership focused on a combination of good results and concern for people. None of these values are exclusively the ownership of women leaders. Men and women are not assumed opposites.

Jean Baker Miller and Irene Pierce Stiver propose an important shift in the view of child development to enhance our understanding of the common importance of relationships. They suggest considering an assessment and appreciation for the ability to enjoy a growing number of healthy relationships as a goal of development rather than individuation.[19] Maturation then is known as the child develops relationships beyond caretakers and family. Understanding child development with a relational focus brings implications for recognizing maturation in women. Women's high value of relationships is not a negative dependency but a positive growth. Men are also potentially encouraged to grow in a connected rather than separated system. For Miller and Stiver, the necessity of "growth-fostering" relationships was not understood as exclusively female.[20] These authors emphasized the importance of studying women to unearth values and experiences missing when only male subjects are used:

> In the present book we are not talking about the questions of sex or gender differences *per se*. Our concern is not how different or similar men and women are. Instead, we have set out to accurately describe women's experience—a still-neglected realm—so as to highlight the fact that certain psychological activities that are vital to the health of all human beings occur in growth-fostering relationships.[21]

While no assumption is to be made regarding men and women being opposites, honoring the fact that all women are not the same is also of importance. Elisabeth Hayes and Daniele D. Flannery are very careful to draw this distinction. They do not want women's studies to polarize assumptions regarding the opposite gender or portray that all women speak in one voice from one experience. They do believe that women must be a focus group for study because of their unique perspective and experiences. The value of studying women exclusively is that concerns and strengths that might not arise in a study of men leaders will be named and potentially recognized by male colleagues.[22]

While women's studies affirm consistently a need among women for connection in relationship and learning, women are not limited to a particular kind of learning. For every generalized theme there are exceptions of women who break these molds. Singular classifications are limited in describing women's diverse experiences and values. Further studies would be of interest to see the effect of assertiveness, competition, and other typically masculine traits becoming more acceptable in women and determining if the high value of relationships among women would change as a result.

I was teaching a class right after students had attended a chapel service in which the speakers had talked about men's and women's needs in relationships. An analogy was used for women's thought and communication style being like spaghetti and men's communication style like waffles. Women, the speakers said, were people of connection, their stories were complicated because everything was important, and if they were troubled in one area of life, it affected all areas of life. Men, on the other hand, compartmentalized. Their needs were simple and did not necessarily feel connected to each other. A male student came in shaking his head and said with some humor and distress, "I'm a woman."

There are real problems with broad generalizations. There are continuums of qualities, experiences, and expressions for men and women. Yet we do live gendered lives. Therefore there are some formative experiences by nurture or nature that I share with other women.

Several studies have revealed a high value of relationships among women. The point is not to deny this value in the lives of men. Generally relationships arose as having higher importance among more women. For women and men leaders who are highly relational there will be a need to find ways to combine that value with effective leadership.

Ann Brooks points out that women's acceptance of themselves as predominantly relational can leave them "unprepared to compete and protect themselves in the larger society."[23]

Fear of speaking, leading, or disrupting relationships can be a great inhibitor as women step into roles that demand these new ways of being. Many women in leadership feel deeply the isolation that comes with high responsibility. I have seen some return to lower positions, not because they were inadequate in their leadership but because they missed the larger camaraderie of having colleagues with whom to share life freely. Certainly part of that isolation is the preponderance of men in those levels of leadership. Again, this is not to say that men cannot be good supportive friends, but there are times when a woman needs another woman, and conversely a man needs to have time with another man. We need to make space for good friendships to flourish. This feeds our souls, adds support to the work environment, and helps us thrive. The challenge is to be fair-minded in practices and assignments in the work environment. As leaders, we need to find ways to develop friendships outside the workplace so not all our supports are shaken during tough times at work.

Fear can plague a woman in learning and leading situations. When working in an environment that has been predominantly male, a woman carries the additional weight of feeling she has to do more than the men in order to earn respect. Another weight is the feeling she won't be allowed time to grow in knowledge and practice of this new position. A breakthrough woman leader will often feel as if she must present herself as invulnerable and all-knowing to fully claim legitimacy to her new position.

The creation of safe places of learning is an initial step toward encouraging women's growth and development. Women must be empowered to function in more challenging milieus. When speaking of training a woman for a nontraditional profession, Jane Hugo suggests significant additional steps are necessary:

> If the workplace is the instructional context, an instructor in charge of teaching women a job (like carpentry or asbestos removal) that has not been a traditional one for women should at least acknowledge the structural barriers women

will face in those occupations and the gendered aspects of many women's level of confidence. As a result of such awareness, instructors could build in more frequent review points and set up a buddy system for women to ensure knowledge transfer once they are out on actual worksites.[24]

A positive instructional context has often been lacking in a woman leader's experience. The honest naming of structural barriers frees a woman to prepare and understand some of the restrictions she is experiencing. Furthermore, the need for more intentional mentorship is clearly necessary as this person overcomes issues of confidence and knowledge acquisition. A women's learning is intertwined with self-concept,[25] and a positive self-concept has implications for leadership. Whether that leadership is from the top or the center, a woman must see her viewpoints as valid and see herself as valuable and skilled.

# ELEVEN

# OBSTACLES

*The love of God is this, that we obey his commandments.*
*And his commandments are not burdensome, for whatever is*
*born of God conquers the world. And this is the victory, our faith.*
*Who is it that conquers the world but the one who believes*
*that Jesus is the Son of God?*

—1 John 5:3-5

꣠꣠꣠

Every person—every leader—faces obstacles in this life, both internal and external. It is difficult at times to discern which came first. Did my expressed lack of confidence come from a naturally shy personality, or was it created by a negative social milieu?

I remember taking swimming lessons at a local pool when I was a child. The setting itself was intimidating; there was a lot of noise as groups of students and teachers splashed in the pool, and the teachers were all yelling instructions at the same time. I was there to take the final swimming test that I had to pass in order to graduate to the next level, and I failed. I remember feeling so defeated. When my mother asked the swimming teacher why I had failed, she was informed that I could do the skills but did not perform them with enough confidence to pass. Years later, when I failed my New York driving test (and there were multiple times I failed the test), the instructor informed my mother that he thought I lacked the confidence to safely operate an automobile.

It's true that I am not a risk-taker, so I am initially hesitant in many ventures. That hesitancy is gradually overcome as I experience people, places, and situations. The environment of my elementary and high school years was rough for me. That atmosphere caused me to keep to myself and watch others closely. Because of my internal tendencies and the external reinforcements, I could easily have become a person with a narrowly prescribed life.

Yet my life has been surprisingly filled with moments of risks, pushing through boundaries and unforeseen adventures. One of the chief reasons it turned out that way is the emphasis my church placed on being fully surrendered to God. Early in my life I knew about God's calling on the lives of his people. Sunday School lessons taught me that this calling was placed upon average people who were hesitant and lacked confidence but were faithfully obedient. When my self-confidence was at its lowest I knew that if I was obedient God would do something wonderful through even me. My obedience led me down a fairly simple path of saying yes to God.

During my college years I was prayerfully and perhaps somewhat obsessively seeking to discern God's will for my life. I experienced an epiphany that illumined my path. While I was in college I visited an elderly woman in a local nursing home just about every week. To be honest, my motivation for visiting her was pity and a sense of duty.

The woman was someone very important to my mother. She had been a literature professor and the academic dean at Eastern Nazarene College and was known for her brilliance, her challenging classroom, and her Christian commitment. By the time I was visiting her she was in her mid-nineties and often confused. She remembered my mother well, though, and once she was reminded that I was Ann's daughter, she settled into her corner easy chair and shared stories. The amazing thing was how often her stories were a clear response to my seeking. In the midst of seeking to know God's call in my life,

Bertha Munro talked about the ways in which God led her to pour her life into Christian higher education. She said it was not a single moment of revelation but that God's leading came through small steps of her obedience. Ultimately, she said that we worry about the huge decisions and forget that the small steps will lead us. She said the journey is one of trusting and obeying God. I still remember her sitting in the corner of her room in the nursing home on an old, flowered, wingback chair with the sun streaming in from the window. There was such peace in her face as she looked at me and sang while marching out the beat with her slippered feet, "Trust and Obey, for there's no other way to be happy in Jesus but to trust and obey."[1]

Five years ago I wouldn't have considered my present position an option for the future. But life is surprising, and the journey brings unexpected twists. Through it all my commitment has been to be faithful to what is revealed in the moment and releasing the unknown future to God's care and revelation.

This journey has allowed me to slowly grow and learn and become a more confident person. The walk of obedience to God's call has allowed me to stretch professionally and academically, which, in turn, has developed my self-assurance. When I was very young there were people who noticed only how scared I was, but there were others who noticed there was a glimmer of hope and possibility. I also enjoyed great support from my family. With all of that, I still think my uncertainties and fears would have remained strong and restricted me if I had not fallen in love with God and, more importantly, discovered God's great love for me.

If you were to look at my baby book, you would see that my first outing after I came home from the hospital was to church. While the church was not a perfect place, it was a loving place. "Jesus Loves Me" was the first song I can remember singing.

I also recall an assignment from a Sunday School teacher to draw our image of God. My drawing was a glowing being, not specifically male or female, on a throne that emanated rays of love. What I discovered as I grew in faith is the more I dwelled in God's love the freer I was to love others and love myself. This assurance is not unwavering, yet it is deep, and even in the hardest times has not been extinguished. In fact, it has been when I felt broken and powerless that I have discovered the love of God that forgives, accepts, heals, and fills.

I also know that I have not begun to grasp the depth and width and height of God's love. My confidence can still be shaken when challenges call upon new or deepened skills and abilities. Critical e-mails of a sermon or a leadership decision I made still challenge my confidence. But these challenges and criticisms don't reach the core of who I am.

When God's love is embedded in the core of my being, strength rises to help me overcome obstacles, endure chaos, and remain steady in times of great uncertainty. As the passage from 1 John says, the world is conquered:

> The love of God is this, that we obey his commandments. And his commandments are not burdensome, for whatever is born of God conquers the world. And this is the victory that conquers our world, our faith. Who is it that conquers the world but the one who believes that Jesus is the Son of God? *(1 John 5:3-5).*

This passage doesn't refer only to conquering external enemies; it includes conquering everything that keeps us from loving God, loving others, and loving ourselves. In this context "conquers the world" does not imply that I now rule the world. Rather, it affirms that the world does not rule over me. Ultimately, for a Christian leader, it is this freedom from the world and the ethos of love that brings us through the internal and external obstacles of life.

Many women in the Church are hesitant to consider themselves able because of a dearth of female role models of leadership—pastoral or otherwise—has presented them with the subtle obstacle of having been offered the model of subversive influence.

"He may be the head, but I am the neck that turns the head" is a quote from the film *My Big Fat Greek Wedding* that exemplifies the role women have typically held in the Church. This indirect authority has left women trained in indirect conversations that are often considered manipulative. It takes intentional insight and work to break old patterns of communication. Grace is needed as a woman grows in her ability to speak her mind directly to others.

The differing communication styles of men and women can sometimes lead to misunderstandings. This would also be true cross-culturally. Diversity of race, cultural background, and gender can strengthen an entity, but intentional communication regarding shared power, process, and outcomes is necessary. The ability to communicate well is an essential skill for all leaders, and as their ability to communicate well grows, they are better able to connect, persuade, and encourage those they lead.

It is not uncommon for a woman leader to believe she gave a directive, but her softer language is heard as a suggestion. A man may think he is making his argument clear, but the woman who hears it may understand his language as an attempt to control. The move toward better communication skills by leaders requires openness to the feedback of the people they lead.

Another obstacle often cited by women is the "old boys' network." Interestingly, women I interviewed were hesitant to name this as a concern. Initially they talked about the acceptance they had received from their denomination's local structure. One of the terms used by women pastors was that they were "home grown." They had been trained through a course of study that allowed them to remain in their local church and worked with senior pastors who had significant oversight of the ordination process and the woman's ultimate placement.

One of the women I interviewed was "home grown" and was supported by her leadership until she began to grow and thrive and gain some national attention. Then her support began to fade rather quickly. There wasn't an overt confrontation, but the larger opportunities to speak and lead were slowly stripped away. She initially assumed this was the natural course of life's ebb and flow. Eventually conversations and directives were exposed that revealed a much more intentional decision to limit her influence.

Other women I spoke with found the significance of the work they were doing was downplayed and whatever growth occurred under their leadership was attributed to odd events aside from the women's gifts as leaders.

Many times, a woman leader's husband was the brunt of comments made at gatherings for pastors and spouses. There were jokes made about his role within his family and who drove the car to the gathering. These comments conveyed a deep message of non-acceptance. ) Husband

A woman in leadership is often faced with the fact that her position of authority causes discomfort within the organization she serves. Sometimes a person who works for a female leader is diminished in his or her own strengths and abilities simply because he or she works for a woman. )

A woman who has the distinction of being the first female to achieve a position of authority in an organization may encounter resistance as her leadership develops. It can be particularly difficult for a man if a woman he initially endorsed and encouraged rises to a level that puts her in a position of authority over him. His reaction can be to second guess her leadership decisions and try to create a general lack of support for her initiatives. It can be a difficult transition from being the one who graciously opens the door for a woman to lead and then discover that he is now under authority.

In every organization there can be subtle ways in which women are not included in important decision-making processes. Women are often offered the first steps to inclusion but then limited the access to be a part of real change.

A general assessment of committees and decision-making boards in Christian organizations continue to reflect a predominantly male presence. Leadership must reflect the membership of the organization. It is also important that when women are given the opportunity to serve in leadership roles that they step up and serve. Of course, there are instances where personal health or other commitments make serving impossible, but it is hard for women to confront the lack of gender balance within an organization when the nominating committee can name fifteen women who turned down invitations to participate.

A Christian woman in leadership is often asked to defend her gifts, calling, and leadership against certain passages of scripture. She must have some ability to explain her understanding of the more controversial passages regarding women in leadership. It is helpful to have some skills in describing tools for interpretation or even that interpretation is done with all passages. Those who want to use 1 Timothy has a hammer against women must  ask themselves why they are not following other passages so literally.

It is beyond the scope of this book to do a comprehensive study of difficult passages concerning women. Several good texts take the authority of God's Word and tackle more problematic passages.[2] It is incumbent upon women to be knowledgeable of the passages that support women in leadership.[3] It is also vital that both men and women read the Scriptures as a whole regarding the call to discipleship, surrender, and the grace that is available to all.

My call did not come about through the passages that affirm women in leadership. My call was in response to the breadth of Scripture that called me to follow Christ with all of my being.

It was not until God called me to pastor that I was asked to defend myself against passages that were interpreted to prohibit female leadership. This demanded my wrestling with scripture as a whole rather than just 1 Timothy 2:11-15. These particular verses from 1 Timothy will never be my life verses, but I am now able to read them and understand them in ways that are much fuller than a demand for women to be silent.

Christian women leaders may find themselves at the center of controversy. In my first senior pastorate my church was asked to not participate in the annual Thanksgiving Evangelical Ecumenical Service because I, the pastor, was a woman. Granted, some other churches declined to take part in the service when this became known. The headlines of the local paper reported "Women's Ordination Issue Splits Lynn-Area Churces."[4]

While this was the most public challenge to my position, I continue to live with the controversial nature of my call to the pastorate. The reality is, though, that negative reactions have not been detrimental to my overall work. I find it interesting that those most critical of my leadership are generally those who are not directly affected by it. The complaints and arguments most often come from Christian brothers and sisters in other organizations.

I do get weary of defending my call, and I now refer my detractors to books they can read if they are truly interested in understanding my biblical stance. I find this preferable to engaging in lengthy conversations.

Every leader faces obstacles. The challenge is to discover the skills, support, power, and process to overcome them. There are common leadership skills to be learned that can be found in leadership books and class syllabus. The extra layer for women is to give themselves the space to apply those lessons to the context of their particular challenges, their lives as woman leaders, and who they serve. In the worst of days we are called to breathe deeply of God's love and grace while believing God is faithful to lead us forward.

TWELVE

# NECESSARY QUALITIES

*The fruit of the Spirit is love, joy, peace, patience, kindness, generosity,*
*faithfulness, gentleness, and self-control. There is no law against such*
*things. And those who belong to Christ Jesus have crucified the flesh*
*with its passions and desires. If we live by the Spirit,*
*let us also be guided by the Spirit.*
—Galatians 5:22-25

❧❧❧

❧ All Christians, and especially those in leadership, are to manifest the fruit of the Spirit in their lives. All of us know that we continue to grow in bearing this fruit, and we could probably name at least one that we find more challenging to exhibit than the others. I'm sure that very few of us would claim to have conquered patience. Yet I know that I am more patient through the work of the Holy Spirit in my life then I would be on my own. Evidence of the work of the Holy Spirit in the life of a person has a far more profound impact on leadership abilities than gender.

In a qualitative study of common characteristics among successful women pastors, I discovered six descriptive themes: godly, passionate, relational/loving/kind, hardworking, persistent, and intelligent.[1] These intertwine in important ways. The passion of the pastor influences the perception of the godliness. The consistent actions of love and kindness make way for good relationships. Their persistence is augmented by their willingness to work hard. I would argue that these qualities are expressions of the fruit of the spirit and are necessary for effective leadership in all realms.

In the above-mentioned study of women pastors, godliness was mentioned most often in the interviews and question-naires. It is important that Christian leaders' lives be worthy of emulation. There may be messy edges to their lives, and they will not be perfect, but they should live with integrity and be good examples. Christian leaders should support their people in difficult days and rejoice with them for good days. During a cross campus initiative one university paired faculty and staff into prayer partners. A member of the custodial staff shared that it was significant for him to spend time in prayer with the university president. This kind of godly presence goes a long way in creating positive regard and trust for the leadership.

Godliness is also made evident in leaders' humble spir-its. Christian leaders must think more highly of others than of themselves, seek the common good, show commitment with-out regard to position or prestige, and emulate moral strength and integrity. Christian leaders are very aware that they are in need of grace as are all others. They also understand that they are dependent upon God for the fulfillment of their leader-ship roles. It is important that people who come in contact with Christian leaders see the leader as someone who truly cares about all volunteers and employees.

For those in pastoral leadership, weekly worship provides the opportunity to share ways God is at work in their lives. Each of the pastors in the study was described as being filled with the spirit. Even when the lay leaders felt the morning worship expe-rience needed improvement, they were in awe of the ways their pastors were led and used by God's spirit. Interestingly, when a pastor used the pulpit to confess personal shortcomings, the perception of the pastor's godliness increased.

Effective Christian leaders must be passionate about the work God has called them to do. This passion is intertwined with experiencing God's strengthening, enduring, faithful work in and through their lives. Passion for God and vocation enhances leaders' ability to express all they believe can happen through the success of their particular organization. This passion can be expressed in a variety of ways according to the leader's personality. Whether the leaders are boisterous or quiet, those who work with them need to know they care deeply about their work.

A Christian leader will care about relationships, although this concern cannot outweigh decisions that need to be made for the good of the organization. The Christian leader must use wisdom in personnel decisions as well as instructing, collaborating, and giving direction to employees. It is important that the Christian leader invests in healthy relationships personally and professionally. Consistency in being loving and kind are the foundations of positive leadership.

Christian leaders should accept people in a way similar to what Greenleaf called "acceptance," which was an expression of love that also encouraged growth and change.[2] This is consistent with Greenleaf's emphasis on servant leadership, which is the ability to listen, understand, and communicate.[3] Spiritual leadership flows from the love the leaders had for their people.[4]

Paul exemplifies this love in his letter to the church of Philippi. He begins the letter saying, "I long for all of you with the compassion of Christ Jesus" (Philippians 1:8). Later he again refers to his love for them: "Therefore, my brothers and sisters, whom I love and long for, my joy and crown, stand firm in the Lord in this way, my beloved" (Philippians 4:1).

Endurance, or persistence, is a necessary characteristic of every leader. The leader must be resolute in grappling with tough issues to help the organization fulfill its mission. For the Christian leader, this strength to persist primarily arises from the leader's relationship to God. In Philippians 2:1-11 the phrase "encouragement [paraklesis] in Christ" refers to the courage available to the community and, therefore, the individual to fulfill the call of God on his or her life. The power to persist is based on leaders' willingness to lean on God's strength and wisdom in the tough times. The basis for the undefeatable hope among the pastors I studied was the power of the resurrection at work in the lives of their churches and the promise of the Holy Spirit's infilling strength and guidance. Whenever looking at future obstacles the pastors believed firmly that God was able to bring them through. Similar to what was observed in Paul's life, leaders need this combination of power or persistence based on the resurrection and a willingness to serve and sacrifice based on the incarnation (Philippians 2:1-11; 3:10-11; Ephesians 1:19-23).

Hope in the midst of daunting realities is necessary for the Christian leader who is attempting to bring a body of people to a new level of church vitality. Faith combined with the power of the Holy Spirit continues to feed the leader the ferocious resolve needed to lead a church into the future. This kind of community change is a difficult but necessary task for the ongoing effectiveness and ability to fulfill mission.

While hope and determination are important, it is also necessary for the leader to be realistic about what is going on within the organization. Failure can come not because it was inevitable but because the danger of going under was acknowledged too late. I have sat with church boards that have lost twenty-five to fifty percent of their membership and still consider the church to be a healthy church. Being honest about the circumstances and challenges a church faces helps a Christian leader remain faithful to the call to lead in challenging times. Acknowledging that an organization is in trouble can be daunting, yet words of honest assessment can mark the beginning of a turnaround that ultimately saves an organization from death. There is hope through God's activity in our lives and organizations that will help us face the harsh realities. Blind hope without truth is ineffective leadership and leads to closings and frustrations.

Throughout Paul's letters to the Early Church, he faced tough challenges that surrounded him, but he never lost hope. He trusted God's provision and work in and through each situation. He was called to be faithful and true. He faced brutal realities throughout Philippians. In the first chapter he is open about his upcoming trial and those who were ministering with mixed motives (Philippians 1:12-18). Paul faced a harsh truth in Philippians 2 and talks about the potential of death or freedom as a result of the trial. Philippians 3 begins with a strong warning against persons and teachings that could harm the believers; and in Philippians 4 Paul names difficulties among members. These examples represent the brutally honest statements seen throughout this letters.

Christian leaders sometimes cling to faithfulness but forget to include honesty, responsiveness to the truth that is revealed in that honesty, and the pursuit of God's direction in the light of that truth. Paul's assurance and the resolve he desires for the church was made evident in his prayer found in Philippians 3:21—4:1:

> He will transform the body of our humiliation that it may be conformed to the body of his glory, by the power that also enables him to make all things subject to himself. Therefore, my brothers and sisters, whom I love and long for, my joy and crown, stand firm in the Lord in this way, my beloved.

Paul calls people to a true understanding of who they are, to name the challenges they face or will face, and to focus their energies toward service and commitment to Christ. He challenges, "Let those of us then who are mature be of the same mind; and if you think differently about anything, this too God will reveal to you. Only let us hold fast to what we have attained" (Philippians 3:15-16). With honesty, Paul met myriad challenges and in doing so maintained an undefeatable hope.

For Paul this call to power is based on his understanding that the power at work in the resurrection of Jesus Christ is at work in the lives of those who follow Christ. In his letter to the Ephesians his prayer reflects this belief:

> That power is like the working of his mighty strength, which he exerted in Christ when he raised him from the

dead and seated him at his right hand in the heavenly realms, far above all rule and authority, power and dominion, and every title that can be given, not only in the present age but also in the one to come *(Ephesians 1:19-21, NIV).*

Obviously this is a hope that surpasses the thriving success of any particular church or organization. The Christian leader is called to ultimately know that even when failure does come, life in Christ surpasses the particular circumstances.

Wisdom is a broad category that embraces intelligence, discernment, knowledge, good judgment, and skill. All of these are important aspects of an effective leader. This wisdom is known in foresight, strategic thinking, and clear communication. The pastors I studied were described by their people with words such as intelligent, smart, and wise. Some of the pastors did not have a high value of their own intelligence. Their intuitive good leadership skills and innovative approaches to ministry were not always self-affirmed, a finding similar to common feminist thought that found women felt devalued when their knowledge base did not fit into the higher educational systems. Three of them held a high school education as their highest degree. When describing their learning processes they were taught largely by on–the-job training. They all had significant pastors in their lives who believed in them, invested in their leadership growth, and continued to serve as mentors.

A significant sign of their growth was movement from receiving and enacting the knowledge from the mentor to the construction of their own sense of knowledge that continued to integrate and question what was received with their new learning through studies and experience.[5] These women expressed increased confidence when their knowledge base was experienced, named, and confirmed within a network of relationships. As this confidence in their knowledge base grew so did the confidence of their congregations.

Growing in wisdom and stature is an ongoing challenge for leaders. The dynamics of organizations, churches, or businesses have been changing at an unparalleled pace. Leaders must be generalists on many subjects: finance, legal requirements, technology, new currents, and innovative responses. Yet they must also hold deeply to the most important things. For a Christian leader this includes a life that in all circumstances bears fruit: "love, joy, peace, patience, kindness, generosity, faithfulness, gentleness and self-control" (Galatians 5:22-23).

These standards can be daunting, but Christian leaders may find hope, for fruit of the Spirit is not produced in one's own strength. It comes to us through the indwelling power of the Holy Spirit. Our hope is in God, and He is at work within us.

It is impossible to talk about the necessary qualities for Christian leadership without addressing the centrality of a life committed to Jesus Christ, lived by the power of the Holy Spirit, to the glory and service of God. All life-giving attributes flow from this core.

With this said, I think it is a faithful and positive expression of this Spirit-led life to critique the many ways women are hindered from fulfilling their potential as leaders in and outside of the church. The challenge is to keep the passion of our work centered on living out the gospel in the midst of those tensions.

Christian leadership has this radical optimism that believes God can do amazing things in us, through us, and around us. For women who have the gift of leadership there is a necessity to lead—not because of some compulsion but because the call of God is upon them. The call of discipleship is to speak, move out of the expected places, and follow Christ with wholehearted obedience. May God's people, male and female, be freed to exercise their gifts that will truly bring glory to God.

There is a beautiful corporate prayer found in Colossians 1:9-14. It is important that any gender, race, and name can be inserted into the "you" and the prayer will still ring true. This prayer is offered to every member of the church, including women and men in leadership.

*For this reason, since the day we heard it, we have not ceased praying for you and asking that you may be filled with the knowledge of God's will in all spiritual wisdom and understanding, so that you may lead lives worthy of the Lord, fully pleasing to him, as you bear fruit in every good work and as you grow in the knowledge of God. May you be made strong with all the strength that comes from his glorious power, and may you be prepared to endure everything with patience, while joyfully giving thanks to the Father, who has enabled you to share in the inheritance of the saints in the light. He has rescued us from the power of darkness and transferred us into the kingdom of his beloved Son, in whom we have redemption, the forgiveness of sins. [Amen.]*

# NOTES

## Chapter 1

1. Ched Myers, *Binding the Strong Man; A Political Reading of Mark's Story of Jesus* (Maryknoll, N.Y.: Orbis Books, 1988).

2. Raymond Pickett, "Following Jesus in Galilee: Resurrection as Empowerment in the Gospel of Mark," *Currents in Theology and Mission* 32:6 (December 2005), 438 (1:29-34; 5:21-43; 6:5, 53-56; 7:31-37; 8:22-26; 10:46-52).

3. Joanna Dewey, "Women in the Gospel of Mark," *Word and World* 26:1, winter 2006, 23.

4. Mark 5:34, translated by Donald Juel in *The Gospel of Mark* (Nashville: Abingdon Press, 1999), 115.

5. Susan Lochrie Graham, "Silent Voices: Women in the Gospel of Mark," *Semeia* 54:1 (2006), <http://www.atla.com/titles/titles_atlas.html>

6. <http://www.nazarenepastor.org/cms/Home/WomenClergy/Articles/Timeline/tabid/184/Default.aspx>.

7. Edward Cooke, *The Life of Florence Nightingale* (New York: Macmillan, 1942), 57.

8. Phoebe Palmer, *Promise of the Father* (New York: self-published, 1872), 8.

9. Ibid.

## Chapter 2

1. Susan Stanley, *Holy Boldness: Women Preachers' Autobiographies and the Sanctified Self* (Knoxville, Tenn.: University of Tennessee Press, 2002), 15, 139.

2. Marva Dawn, *Royal Waste of Time* (Grand Rapids: Eerdmans Publishing 1999), 143.

3. Tom Rainer, *Breakout Churches* (Grand Rapids: Zondervan Publishing House, 2005), 87.

4. Ibid.

5. Wesley D. Tracy et al., *The Upward Call* (Kansas City: Beacon Hill Press of Kansas City, 1994), 89.

6. Ibid.

## Chapter 3

1. Examples include Carol Becker, *Becoming Colleagues* (San Francisco: Jossey-Bass, 2000); Sally Helgesen, *The Female Advantage: Women's Ways of Leadership* (New York: Doubleday, 1990); Nancy Goldberger et al., *Knowledge, Difference, and Power: Essays Inspired by Women's Ways of Knowing* (New York: Perseus, 1996).

2. Sue Thomas, "The Impact of Women in Political Leadership Positions," in *Women and American Politics: New Questions, New Directions*, ed. Susan J. Carroll (Oxford: Oxford University Press, 2003).

3. Thomas R. Hawkins, *The Learning Congregation* (Louisville, Ky.: Westminster John Knox Press, 1997), 49.

4. Ibid.

5. Joseph E. Coleson, *Ezer Cenegdo: A Power like Him, Facing Him as Equal,* (Wesleyan/Holiness Women Clergy, Inc., c/0 Messiah College, Grantham, Pa., 1996). <http://www.whwomenclergy.org/booklets/power_like_him.php>.

6. Ibid., 12.

7. Ibid., 5.

8. Ruth Haley Barton, *Equal to the Task: Men & Women in Partnership* (Downers Grove, Ill.: InterVarsity Press, 1998), 22.

9. Ibid.

## Chapter 4

1. Henri Nouwen, *The Return of the Prodigal: A Story of Homecoming* (New York: Doubleday, 1994) 108.

2. Diane Leclerc, "Singleness of Heart: Gender, Sin, and Holiness," in *Historical Perspective* (London: The Scarecrow Press, 2001), 156.

3. I am indebted to Diane Leclerc's work in the cited text above.

4. George Williamson, *Noble Purpose,* song used at Point Loma Nazarene University chapel service. Used by permission.

5. Christopher Joyce, "Mosquito Duet Leads to Love," National Public Radio, January 9, 2009, "Morning Edition" program.

## Chapter 5

1. Henri Nouwen, *The Wounded Healer* (New York: Doubleday, 1972), 27.

2. Rainer, *Breakout Churches,* 87.

3. Ibid., 87.

4. David Hansen, *The Art of Pastoring: Ministry Without All the Answers* (Downers Grove, Ill.: Intervarsity Press, 1994) 128.

5. Nouwen, *The Wounded Healer,* 72

6. <http://www.lutheran-hymnal.com/lyrics/hs889.htm>.

7. Nouwen, 38

## Chapter 6

1. Helen Bruch Pearson, *Do What You Have the Power to Do: Studies of Six New Testament Women* (Nashville: Upper Room Books, 1992).

2. Ibid., 64

3. Reinhold Niebuhr, <http://www.cptryon.org/prayer/special/serenity.html>.

4. Pearson, *Do What You Have the Power to Do,* 50

5. Stanley, *Holy Boldness,* 98.

6. Thomas Jay Oord and Michael Lodahl, *Relational Holiness: Responding to the Call of Love* (Kansas City: Beacon Hill Press of Kansas City, 2005), 73.

## Chapter 7

1. John Emerich, Edward Dalberg Acton, first Baron Acton (1834–1902) expressed this opinion in a letter to Bishop Mandell Creighton in 1887. Accessible at <http://www.phrases.org.uk/meanings/22900.html>.

2. Hansen, *The Art of Pastoring*, 68.

3. Cheryl Forbes, *Are We Victims of the Religion of Power?* (Grand Rapids: Zondervan Publishing House, 1983), 20.

4. Ibid., 157.

5. Ibid., 68.

6. Ibid., 180.

7. Calvin Miller, *The Empowered Leader: 10 Keys to Servant Leadership* (Nashville: Broadman and Holman, 1995), 130.

8. Galinsky, McGee, Inesi and Gruenfeld, *Psychological Science*, 17:12 (December 2006), 1068-1074.

9. Ibid., 1072

10. LifeWay Christian Resources.

11. VBS 2004 FAQ (Frequently Asked Questions), Far-Out Far East Rickshaw Rally: Racing for the Son, <http://www.lifeway.com>.

12. <http://www.geocities.com/reconsideringrickshawrally/>.

13. Ibid., 1068.

14. Peter Scazzero with Warren Bird, *The Emotionally Healthy Church* (Grand Rapids: Zondervan Publishing House, 2003), 20-32.

15. Ibid., 37

16. J. Oswald Sanders, *Spiritual Leadership: Principles of Excellence for Every Believer* (Chicago: Moody Press, 1994).

17. Ibid., 154

28. Carol Becker, *Leading Women* (Nashville: Abingdon Press, 1996), 164.

19. Forbes, *Are We Victims of the Religion of Power?* 24.

20. Becker, *Becoming Colleagues*, 257.

21. Thomas Hawkins, *Faithful Leadership* (Nashville: Discipleship Resources, 2001), 58.

## Chapter 8

1. Andre'Comté-Sponville, *A Small Treatise on the Great Virtues* (New York: Metropoliton Books, 1996), 147.

2. Raymond J. Deverette, *Introduction to Virtue Ethics* (Washington, D.C.: Georgetown UP, 2002), 77.

3. Thomas à Kempis, *The Imitation of Christ*, ed. Donald E. Demaray (New York: Alba House, 1996), 10.

4. Stephen J. Pope, ed., *The Ethics of Aquinas* (Washington, D.C.: Georgetown UP, 2002), 45.

5. Richard Foster and James Bryan Smith, *Devotional Classics: Selected Readings for Individuals and Groups* (San Francisco: Harper, 1993), 179, 269-70; and George Burch, *Bernard Abbot of Clairvaux: The Steps of Humility* (Notre Dame, Ind.: University of Notre Dame, 1963), 131.

6. Andrew Murray, *Humility* (Springdale, Pa.: Whitaker House, 1982), 12.

7. Augustine, *The Confessions: Introduction, Translation and Notes,* ed. Maria Boulding, O. S. B. and John E. Rotelle (Hyde Park, N.Y.: New City Press, 1997), 276.

8. Ibid., 274.

9. Patout J.Burns, "Augustine on the Origin and Progress of Evil," *The Ethics of St. Augustine,* ed. William Babcock (Atlanta: Scholars, 1991), 82.

10. Lee F. Bacchi, "A Ministry Characterized by and Exercised in Humility: The Theology of Ordained Ministry in the Letters of Augustine of Hippo," *Collectanea Augustiniana,* ed. Joseph T. Linehard, Earl C. Muller, and Roland J. Teske (New York: Peter Lange, 1993) 405.

11. Toal, M. F., ed. *The Sunday Sermons of the Great Fathers, Vol. 2.* (Swedesboro, N.J.: Preservation Press, 1996), 274.

12. Leclerc, "Singleness of Heart," 30.

13. Ibid., 49.

14. Carol LakeyHess, "Reclaiming Ourselves: A Spirituality for Women's Empowerment," in
*Women, Gender, and Christian Community* (Louisville, Ky.: Westminster-John Knox Press,1997), 146.

15. Jim Collins, *Good to Great* (New York: Harper, 2001), 20.

16. Ralph Martin, *A Hymn of Christ* (Downers Grove, Ill.: InterVarsity Press, 1997), 91.

17. Markus Bockmuehl, *Black's New Testament Commentary: The Epistle to the Philippians* (Peabody, Mass.: Hendrickson Publishers, 1998), 110.

18. Ibid., 129.

19. Ibid., 133.

20. Klaus Wengst *Humility: Solidarity of the Humiliated* (Philadelphia: Fortress Press, 1988), 49.

21. Gerald F. Hawthorne, *Word Biblical Themes: Philippians* (Waco, Tx.: Word, 1987) 73.

22. Markus Bockmuehl, *Black's New Testament Commentary: The Epistle to the Philippians* (Peabody, Mass.: Hendrickson Publishers, 1998), 140.

23. F. Bruce, *New International Biblical Commentary: Philippians* (Peabody, Mass.: Hendrickson Publishers, 1983), 72.

24. Collins, *Good to Great,* 20.

25. Marty Wooten, *Second Corinthians and the Ministry of Paul: Power in Weakness* (Woburn, Mass.: Discipleship Publications International, 1996), 65.

26. Bervard S. Childs, *Biblical Theology of the Old and New Testaments: Theological Reflection on the Christian Bible* (Minneapolis: Fortress Press, 1992), 470.

27. Brian Hebblethwaite, "Jesus, God Incarnate," in *The Truth of God Incarnate,* ed. Michael Green (Grand Rapids: Wm. B. Eerdmans Press, 1977), 102.

## Chapter 9

1. According to Spears, the term was first introduced through Greenleaf's essay published in 1970, which later became a book entitled *The Servant as Leader* (Spears 2).

2. Collins, *Good to Great,* 30.

3. Ibid., 30.

4. Robert Greenleaf, *Servant: Retrospect and Prospect* (Peterborough, N.H.: Windy Row, 1980), 22.

5. Oswald J. Sanders, *Spiritual Leadership* (Chicago: Moody Press, 1967), 15.

6. Ibid., 15.

7. Ibid., 52.

8. Ibid., 28.

9. Henry Blackaby and Richard Blackaby, *Spiritual Leadership* (Nashville: Broadman, 2001), 164.

10. Ibid., 165.

11. Robert Greenleaf, *Servant Leadership* (New York: Paulist Press, 1977), 20.

12. R. Paul Stevens, *The Other Six Days: Vocation, Work, and Ministry in Biblical Perspectives* (Grand Rapids: Eerdsmans, 1999), 135-36.

13. Greenleaf, *Servant Leadership,* 42.

14. David Young, *Servant Leadership for Church Renewal* (Scottsdale, Pa.: Herald Press, 1999), 33-36.

15. Hawkins, *Faithful Leadership,* 57.

16. Ibid., 57.

17. Larry Spears, *Reflections on Leadership* (New York: John Wiley, 1995). Also Larry Spears and Michelle Lawrence, *Focus on Leadership: Servant-Leadership for the 21st Century* (New York: John Wiley, 2002).

18. Spears and Lawrence, *Focus on Leadership,* 14.

19. Lois P. Frankel, *Nice Girls Don't Get the Corner Office: 101 Unconscious Mistakes Women Make That Sabotage Their Careers* (New York: Warner Business, 2004), 87.

20. Becker, *Leading Women,* 169.

21. Ibid., 145.

22. Sarah Sumner, *Men and Women in the Church: Building Consensus on Christian Leadership* (Downers Grove, Ill.: InterVarsity Press, 2003), 74-75.

23. Becker, *Leading Women,* 162.

24. Ibid., 164

25. Becker, *Becoming Colleagues*, 254.

26. Becker, *Leading Women*, 165.

27. Bennet Sims, *Servanthood: Leadership for the Third Millenium* (Boston: Cowley, 1997), 29.

28. Young, *Servant Leadership*, 14.

29. Sims, *Servanthood*, 90.

### Chapter 10

1. Becker, *Becoming Colleagues*, 91.

2. Ibid., 88.

3. Carol Gilligan, *In a Different Voice* (Cambridge, Mass.: Harvard University Press, 1982).

4. Nancy Goldberger et al., *Knowledge, Difference, and Power: Essays Inspired by Women's Ways of Knowing* (New York: Perseus, 1996), 7.

5. Ibid., 7.

6. Mary Field Belenky et al., *Women's Ways of Knowing: The Development of Self, Voice and* Mind (New York: Perseus, 1986), vii.

7. Karen Lee Ashcraft and Michael E. Pacanowsky, "A Women's Worst Enemy, Reflections on a Narrative of Organizational Life and Female Identity," *Journal of Applied Communication Research* 24, (Aug. 1996): 217-39.

8. Sumner, *Men and Women in the Church*, 52.

9. Becker, *Becoming Colleagues*, 10.

10. Deborah Tannen, *You Just Don't Understand: Women and Men in Conversation* (New York: William and Morrow, 1990).

11. Ibid., 228.

12. Leonora Tubbs Tisdale, "Women's Ways of Communicating," in *Women, Gender, and Christian Community*, ed. Jane Dempsey Douglass and James F. Kay (Louisville: Westminster-John Knox Press, 1997), 109.

13. Tannen, 240.

14. Frankel, 88.

15. Sally Helgesen, *The Female Advantage: Women's Ways of Leadership* (New York: Doubleday, 1990), 22.

16. Ibid., 46.

17. Ibid., 30.

18. Ibid., 31.

19. Jean Baker Miller and Irene Pierce Stiver, *The Healing Connection: How Women Form Relationships in Therapy and in Life* (Boston: Beacon Press, 1997), 15.

20. Ibid., 22.

21. Ibid., 21.

22. Elisabeth Hayes and Daniele D. Flannery, *Women as Learners* (San Francisco: Jossey-Bass, 2000) 19.

23. Ann Brooks, "Transformation" in Elisabeth Hayes and Daniele D. Flannery, *Women as Learners* (San Francisco: Jossey-Bass, 2000), 143.

24. Jane Hugo, "Perspectives on Practice," in Hayes and Flannery, *Women as Learners,* 197.

25. Hayes and Flannery, *Women as Learners,* 238.

## Chapter 11

1. *Sing to the Lord,* (Kansas City: Lillenas Publishing House, 1993) 437.

2. C. S. Cowles, *A Women's Place? Leadership in the Church* (Kansas City: Beacon Hill Press, 1993); Aida Besancon Spencer, *Beyond the Curse: Women Called to Ministry* (Peabody, Mass.: Hendrickson Press, 1985; Richard Clark Kroeger and Catherine Clark Kroeger, *Rethinking 1 Timothy 2:11-15 in Light of Ancient Evidence: I Suffer Not a Woman* (Grand Rapids: Baker Books, 1992).

3. Acts 2:17-21, Joel 2:28-32, Romans 16:1-4, Acts 18:24-26, Acts 21:9, Galatians 3:28, to name a few.

4. *Daily Evening,* 227:140, 1.

## Chapter 12

1. Mary Rearick Paul, *The Common Leadership Qualities of Nazarene Women Pastors Who Have Led Good To Great Churches,* (Dissertation, Asbury Theological Seminary, 2005).

2. Greenleaf, *Servant Leadership,* 20.

3. Ibid., 3.

4. Blackaby and Blackaby, *Spiritual Leadership,* 165.

5. Belenky et al., *Women's Ways of Knowing.*

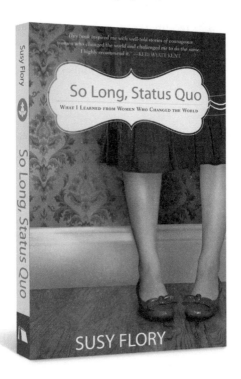

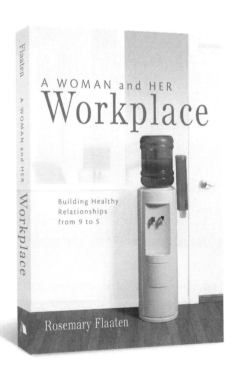

More than a book about how to get along with difficult people, *A Woman and Her Workplace* shows you how to allow God to perform a transformation in your heart that will allow His love and care to flow through you to the people you work alongside. You will learn to recognize and stand against attitudes that wreak havoc on workplace relationships and replace them with strong biblical principles such as humility, integrity, forgiveness, grace, and celebration.

A Woman and Her Workplace
*Building Healthy Relationships from 9 to 5*
Rosemary Flaaten
ISBN: 978-0-8341-2523-0

BEACON HILL PRESS
OF KANSAS CITY

Available online or wherever books are sold.